WINDSURFING

OUTDOOR PURSUITS SERIES

Ken Winner

Human Kinetics

Library of Congress Cataloging-in-Publication Data

Winner, Ken.
  Windsurfing / Ken Winner.
    p.   cm. -- (Outdoor pursuits series)
  Includes index.
  ISBN 0-87322-760-3
  1. Windsurfing. I. Title. II. Series.
GV811.63.W56W535   1995
797.3'3--dc20   94-25210
                                                                               CIP

ISBN: 0-87322-760-3

Copyright © 1995 by Human Kinetics Publishers, Inc.

Developmental Editor: Julia Anderson; **Assistant Editors:** Ed Giles and Jacqueline Blakley; **Copyeditor:** John Wentworth; **Proofreader:** Heather Shupp; **Indexer:** Theresa Schaefer; **Photo Editor:** Boyd LaFoon; **Typesetter:** Ruby Zimmerman; **Text Designer and Layout Artist:** Robert Reuther; **Cover Designer:** Jack Davis; **Cover Photo:** Darrell Jones; **Illustrator:** Thomas • Bradley Illustration & Design; **Printer:** Buxton Skinner

Human Kinetics books are available at special discounts for bulk purchase. Special editions or book excerpts can also be created to specification. For details, contact the Special Sales Manager at Human Kinetics.

Printed in the United States of America   10   9   8   7   6   5   4   3   2   1

Human Kinetics
P.O. Box 5076, Champaign, IL 61825-5076
1-800-747-4457

Canada: Human Kinetics, Box 24040, Windsor, ON N8Y 4Y9
1-800-465-7301 (in Canada only)

Europe: Human Kinetics, P.O. Box IW14, Leeds LS16 6TR, England
(44) 532 781708

Australia: Human Kinetics, 2 Ingrid Street, Clapham 5062, South Australia
(08) 371 3755

New Zealand: Human Kinetics, P.O. Box 105-231, Auckland 1
(09) 309 2259

CONTENTS

1

GOING
WINDSURFING

I was starting to feel weary, old.

During my everyday activities, I seemed to be trudging knee-deep in mud, the weight of work bearing implacably on my back. At every turn there were forms to fill out, taxes to pay, yield signs to obey. Only in my mid-30s, I had to throw away a perfectly good belt and buy a longer one.

How long this might have gone on I don't know. I wasn't thinking clearly enough to determine the cause of the problem. Then I got lucky. By chance, I got a contract to test some windsurfing equipment, which called for 3 weeks in the Caribbean, windsurfing every day.

It was therapeutic work, and the cure began the moment I stepped off the plane. A thick, tropical, trade wind blast took the first layer of dust off my shoulders; the brine-laden air ventilated my brain like smelling salts. The sun was so bright I felt like one of those prisoners in *Fidelio*: walking outdoors slowly, haltingly, softly singing *freiheit, freiheit,* freedom, freedom, unsure what else to do or say.

Friends, fortunately, knew what to do. They led me to the edge of the sea and put my windsurfing gear in my hands. I, who had once windsurfed devoutly and then wandered to other ways, dipped my head back into the water, caught the wind with my sail, and was lifted from the water, born again.

I progressed quickly. My strength and flexibility returned, and my sense of balance grew sharper. Day after day of skimming over aqua waters, windsurfing the swells, and jumping waves slowly erased the decrepitude that had begun to take over my body and mind. I slept easily for the first time in months and woke early in the mornings. My belt seemed longer.

That was a few years ago. I still work, of course, but now I know when to stop working and go windsurfing—usually about 2 or 3 o'clock in the afternoon, when the wind kicks in.

Expert high-wind windsurfers are like flying fish—as much out of the water as in.

HOW WINDSURFING BEGAN

Some say windsurfing was invented in 1958 by an English boy named Peter Chilvers. Others credit an inventor from Pennsylvania named S. Newman Darby, who began building and marketing "sailboards" in the mid-1960s. Most accounts, however, tell of two Californians, an aeronautical engineer named Jim Drake and a computer company executive named Hoyle Schweitzer, who designed and patented a windsurfing craft in the late 1960s. The engineer Drake is credited with solving many of the problems involved in getting the board to sail, whereas the more visionary Schweitzer filed for patents and worked on bringing the invention to market.

The first documented windsurfing craft was designed and built in the mid-1960s by S. Newman Darby.

During the 1970s, Schweitzer produced and marketed his Windsurfer worldwide. Hundreds of thousands were sold, and the sport became a craze in Europe. Dozens of other manufacturers entered the market with their own designs, and the sport broke records for growth. It grew so quickly that in 1984, just 15 years after the patent for Drake and Schweitzer's invention had been granted, windsurfing became the youngest sport ever to be included in the Olympics.

With so many people doing it, windsurfing began to evolve at a faster pace. From Hawaii to Europe to Australia, windsurfers developed new techniques and modified their equipment. Racers in Europe built big boards for light-wind racing, while wave sailors in Hawaii made small, maneuverable boards equipped with footstraps for better wave riding and jumping. By the early 1990s, a professional racing circuit was generating millions of dollars of income for professionals, and windsurfing resorts were doing brisk business in warm, windy places throughout the world.

Windsurfing is now much like snow skiing, but about 30 years less mature: It's an exciting, addicting lifestyle sport that will be even more fun, accessible, and appealing in the future.

Types of Windsurfing

Although windsurfing is basically the simplest form of sailing, it can seem incredibly complicated. Consider, for example, that there are over a thousand different sail designs on the market and at least 200 different board models—enough choices to faze even the best decision maker. This abundance is in part a consequence of the sport's great range—the variety of ways in which people enjoy it—from Olympic-style longboard sailing to slalom cruising to Hawaiian-style wave riding and jumping. In this sense, windsurfing is like snow skiing, with its variations such as alpine, cross country, and snowboarding.

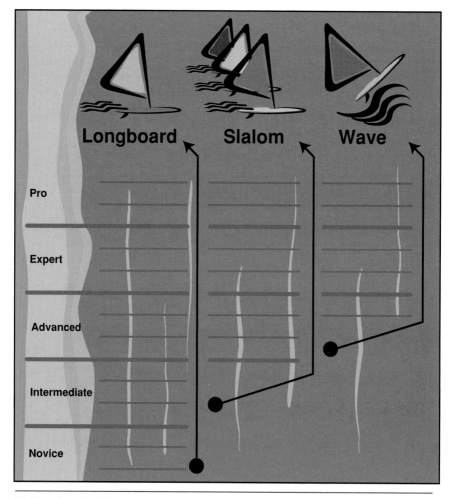

The longboard, slalom, and waveboard branches of the windsurfing tree.

The windsurfing tree has three main branches: longboard, slalom, and wave sailing. Longboards are big, floaty, versatile boards that perform well in most wind and sea conditions. They're used at all levels of ability from beginner to Olympic. The other two branches represent the two main kinds of shortboard sailing: slalom and wave. Shortboards are smaller and less versatile than longboards, and they require more wind. They're not suitable for beginners but are the favorites of many experienced windsurfers who live in, or frequently visit, windy places.

Most windsurfing boards can operate in three modes: The 0- to about 4-mph (0- to 7-kph) displacement mode gives way to the 5- to 12-mph (8- to 20-kph) semiplaning mode, which in turn gives way to the 13- to 50-mph (21- to 83-kph) planing mode as speed increases. Longboards are designed to work well in all modes; shortboards are designed primarily for planing.

What Kind of Windsurfing Is Best for You?

Anyone who wants to get on the water is a prospective windsurfer. If you like to sail but can't afford an actual boat, if you want to enjoy nature in a different way, or if you simply like the idea of holding the wind in your grasp, you should give windsurfing a try. The type of windsurfing that best suits you will depend on the amount of time and money you have to spend, how athletic you are, how much of a challenge you seek in your sports, whether you live in a windy place, and whether there's surf nearby.

Longboard sailing, for example, is accessible to everyone and can be done nearly anywhere. Wave and bump sailing, on the other hand, is for the physically fit thrill-seeker. It's a bit like bump skiing, which requires ample practice in a place with the right conditions. If you're a skier who spends one week a year at Telluride, it's not likely you'll become good enough on your skis to handle big bumps. Likewise, if you can't get 18-mph winds and good waves frequently, you won't make much progress in your wave and bump sailing skills. On the other hand, wave and bump sailing is the most addicting aspect of the sport—the stuff some windsurfers build their lives around. They move to Maui or the Canary Islands and take jobs that leave afternoons free for sailing.

Slalom sailing is perfect if you want to go fast and do high-speed maneuvers but lack the conditions or athleticism for wave and bump sailing. The size, simplicity, quickness to plane, and versatility of a slalom board make it the ideal first shortboard. These same qualities endear it to experts and racers as well. Still, slalom boards require at least 12-mph winds (a bit less for highly skilled experts), which inevitably increases the time and money you have to spend to get a sailing fix.

FIND YOUR WINDSURFING NICHE —

It's important to start right and stay on a path toward windsurfing goals that make sense for you. Let the following questions help you decide what type of windsurfing would suit you best:

1. Do you feel you're not strong or athletic enough to windsurf well? Try sailing a kneesurfer or a big longboard with a small sail in winds under 10 mph. Lack of strength should never be a problem because you can always use a smaller sail.

2. Do you have just one day per week or an hour or two on weekday evenings for windsurfing? Unless you live in a notoriously windy place, like San Francisco, California, or Perth, Australia, your best bet is to concentrate on longboard windsurfing—at least at first.

3. Do you like the idea of competing in a sport that combines the best features of running, gymnastics, chess, and backgammon on levels from beginner to Olympic? The IMCO One Design is the longboard that you can race at any level.

4. Do you want to windsurf because it's a fun way to exercise? IMCO racing offers the best workout if you live in a place that's not particularly windy. Either slalom racing or wave and bump sailing can provide unbeatable workouts if you live near a windy sailing site.

5. Are you an athletic thrill-seeker who lives in a windy place and who can spend plenty of time and money on windsurfing? Dive right in. Learn the basics on a rental longboard, but go ahead and buy a large slalom board and a couple of high-wind sails. Plan to add a wave and bump board and more sails to your collection within a year or two.

SAFETY TIP No matter what type of windsurfing you plan to do or how you plan to get started, learn in places where there are other windsurfers or water users around.

Getting Started

Getting started in windsurfing is not as easy as getting started in cycling. You can't just go to the nearest department store and buy windsurfing equipment the way you can buy a bike, and windsurfing instructors can't be found in most telephone books. Windsurfing is a much more exotic sport than bicycling, and windsurfing shops don't appear on every street. Indeed, many towns and cities lack windsurfing shops entirely. So, where do you go? Check the windsurfing magazines for advertisements about resorts, demonstrations, clubs, clinics, and shops. You're sure to find something that will work for you.

Windsurfing Resorts

Just as most snow skiers go to a ski area to learn skiing, many windsurfers go to a windsurfing resort for their first sail. Instructors at resorts are among the best available, and their equipment is usually top quality. Resort locations are chosen for the congeniality of the weather, so winds are reliable at most resorts and the water warm.

Most resorts offer instructional aids such as special boards and sails, video coaching, and on-land simulators. They also offer quick rescue of windsurfers who find themselves having trouble.

Demonstrations

Various windsurfing manufacturers and retailers often organize "demo days"—on-the-beach opportunities for windsurfers and prospective windsurfers to learn more about the sport and the latest equipment. All comers are welcome to try the gear, take short lessons on dry-land windsurfing simulators, and gab with the experts. Although a demo won't take the place of a week in Aruba, it's free and full of information.

Windsurfing Clubs

Most windsurfing clubs are formed for two main reasons. Some members focus on racing and other social activities, whereas others work primarily to maintain water access. No matter what the focus, windsurfing clubs are great sources of information and camaraderie. They organize events and outings, and the advice you can glean from knowledgeable members can be invaluable. Of course the average club member lacks the extensive experience and wide perspective of a professional instructor, so amateur advice should be only one of your sources of information.

Unlike yacht clubs, few windsurfing clubs own equipment, so you probably won't be able to borrow a club board. Some club members may have gear suitable for novices, however, and are usually eager to lend it out or sell it.

Clinics

Prominent expert and ex-professional windsurfers frequently organize clinics and camps that cater to both experienced and novice windsurfers. In many cases these clinics offer the novice little that's not available in a good resort. Indeed, many take place in windsurfing resorts. But a clinic held at a beach near you can be an inexpensive way to get your feet wet.

Specialty Shops

A windsurfing specialty shop is the obvious place to look for equipment. However, most shops offer lessons, rentals, and demonstrations as well, and the people who run the specialty shops are usually avid windsurfers who will gladly answer any questions. If you doubt what they tell you, keep in mind that they seldom make much money on a customer's first purchase. To make a profit, they need happy, satisfied customers who will return again and again as equipment wears out and improving skills warrant new purchases. In short, specialty shops have every incentive to give you good information, service, and equipment.

A dream job: instructing windsurfing in Aruba.

CONSUMER TIP Specialty shops and windsurfing clubs often host swap meets where windsurfers buy and sell used gear. You don't have to be a buyer to attend one of these events, but you can learn a lot about the local windsurfing scene.

GETTING HOOKED

My first windsurfing session—I mean the first time I actually managed to sail rather than just splash around—took place on a clear, cool day in early April. The winter had stretched well into spring that year, and any sunny day was by then a treasure. On this day the sun was like a small fire in a cold room: Its heat was enough to warm me on one side only. This combined with the wintry chill of the water left me teetering on that thin line between pain and pleasure.

The wind was light, barely strong enough to ripple the surface of the water, so I was able to windsurf for hours and learn some of the basics. In the 20 years since, I've windsurfed thousands of hours and learned much more, but that first session still represents to me the essence of windsurfing. It hinted at the pleasure that comes from the sense of speed, freedom, and accomplishment that are part of windsurfing well. The session gave me an inkling of windsurfing's raw sensuousness: the combination of sensations from sun, sand, wind, and water. It also taught me the pain that comes from mistakes. Of course most errors cause discomfort rather than genuine pain. Whatever the level of discomfort, though, the possibility of it occurring sharpens the senses and heightens the sense of accomplishment when success follows effort. It gives you an unbeatable high—that's how windsurfing caught me.

2

WINDSURFING EQUIPMENT

Windsurfing has the reputation of being a complex, equipment-oriented sport. After all, sailing at 50 mph or jumping 30 feet into the air as the pros do is bound to take some pretty specialized gear. However, at its most basic, windsurfing is really the simplest form of sailing, and the equipment is surprisingly easy to understand and use. Remember how in summer camp you were able to throw on a swimsuit, hop in a canoe, and paddle around without a thought about the equipment involved? Well, the same approach can work in windsurfing. A simple board and rig that costs a few hundred dollars can get you on the water with a minimum of hassle, and, if you venture out in warm weather only, you'll need no attire other than a swimsuit.

Basic windsurfing gear consists of a board with a fin or a fin-centerboard combination attached to the bottom and a rig attached to the top by means of a universal joint. The fin or centerboard is like the keel of a boat: It helps keep the board going forward rather than sideways. The rig is the part that includes the sail; it catches the wind and propels the board. The rig includes a mast, the pole that holds the sail up, and the boom, the part the sailor hangs

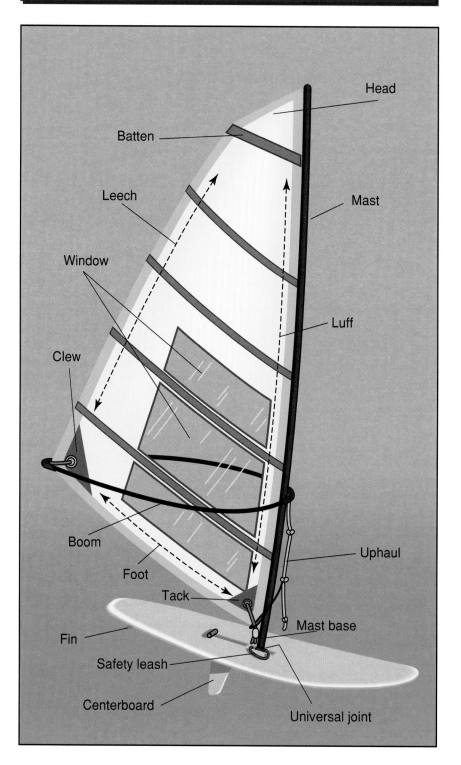

Head

Batten

Leech

Mast

Window

Luff

Clew

Boom

Foot

Uphaul

Tack

Fin

Mast base

Safety leash

Centerboard

Universal joint

on to. The universal joint is the part that makes the board a windsurfing board rather than a conventional sailboat. It allows the rig to swivel and tilt independently of the board and permits the windsurfer to steer by simply angling the sail one way or another.

Choosing the Right Board

Snowboarders choose boards according to their body weight and the type of boarding they plan to do. Likewise with windsurfers. There's no point in having a wave board if you're a novice living in Kansas, and it makes little sense to own a longboard if you're a professional wave sailor in Hawaii.

Kneesurfers

The most basic board is the kneesurfer, which consists of an inflatable board, a big fin (so no centerboard is needed), and an easily assembled rig. A kneesurfer isn't fast, but it's soft and comfortable, easy to transport, and useful for more than just windsurfing. It's good for families looking for a versatile water toy and is appropriate for anyone wanting to learn the basic skills of windsurfing. In short, it suits those who want to taste windsurfing without taking a thousand-dollar bite.

Longboards

Naturally, the most basic equipment is not the most versatile and capable, so as you get more into windsurfing, you'll want to look for a more substantial board. You may even want to start with one. If so, your best bet is a full-featured longboard.

Features

The common features of "full-featured" longboards are their centerboard, foot-adjustable mast track, and footstraps.

The centerboard is different from the fin-only setup of many boards in that it retracts into the board when not needed. Its large size keeps the board from sliding sideways in light winds and at low speeds. However, in strong winds and high speeds, the centerboard is not needed because the fin alone is big enough to take on the job.

Many boards have simple mast tracks, but full-featured longboards have mast tracks that you can adjust while you're actually sailing. You use your front foot to press a lever or button at the back of the track, then slide the foot

Types of Boards

There are three types of windsurfing boards, each appropriate for a specific type of activity.

Kneesurfer

This board is inexpensive, light, collapsible, easy to transport, and easy to rig. A slow board, it's soft and friendly to novices and useful for more than just windsurfing.

Longboard

The most versatile kind of board, the longboard is good for most wind and water conditions. As the type of board used in the Olympics, it features a centerboard, a foot-adjustable mast track, and footstraps. It's the ideal board for windsurfers who live in a place with average wind.

Shortboard

If the wind is strong and the rider skillful, this is the fastest and most maneuverable type of board. It combines simplicity with high-wind performance well beyond that longboards can offer. It features a basic mast track, three or four footstraps, and a high-performance fin.

of the mast forward or back. Why is this sort of track needed? Because of the centerboard. When you raise or lower the centerboard, you change the way the board balances. The foot-adjustable track permits you to move the rig forward or backward to keep the board in balance.

Nearly all boards come with footstraps. Like waterski bindings, straps keep your feet locked in the right places when you're traveling at high speed. Thus, you don't need footstraps in the early stages of learning. Straps can even be a hindrance. Fortunately, you can leave them off the board until the time comes to learn how to use them.

Size

Longboards range from about 10 to 12-1/2 feet (305 to 380 cm) in length and 24 to 31 inches (60 to 79 cm) in width. What size board to buy is a topic of endless debate among windsurfers. However, when it comes to longboards, there are only two credible ways of answering the question.

First, if what you want is the best possible all-around performance in light to moderate wind—and that's the kind of wind most of us see most of the time—the bigger the board, the better. The biggest boards are easiest to stand on and fastest in light winds. They can carry two riders (if you use some ingenuity), and they're great for cruising waterways and seeing the sights.

Second, if the biggest boards available don't appeal to you because of their cost, weight, or bulk, you may opt for something smaller. How small can you go? That depends on your body weight.

Different kinds of longboards are distinguished most usefully not by length but by volume—the amount of space they take up—because a board's volume determines how much weight it can support. The typical longboard is between 140 and 260 liters in volume. Experience has shown that a 220-liter board works well for a 180-pound rider. By extension, then, we can say that a 160-liter board will work well for a 125-pounder, and a 260-liter board will work well for a 220-pounder. See the graph on p. 17. Anyone looking for a good, versatile longboard should consider choosing one with volume at or above the level that the graph indicates is appropriate for his or her weight.

Construction

Longboards come in two main types of construction: poly and composite. Polyboards have a polyethylene or polypropylene skin—similar to the material plastic milk bottles are made of—and a polyurethane foam core. They're heavy but durable and inexpensive. These qualities make them best suited to light-wind sailing and hard use.

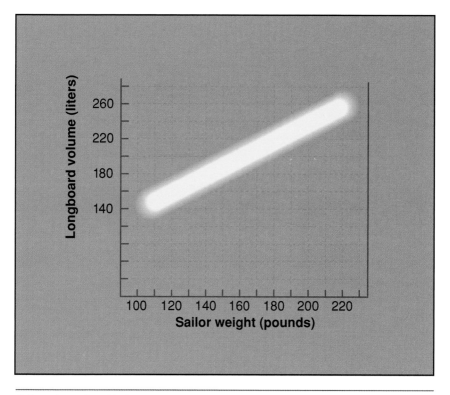

Safe and comfortable longboard volume for novice to intermediate longboard riders.

Composite boards have skins that include materials such as fiberglass, carbon fiber, epoxy resin, honeycomb, and others. Such construction permits composite boards to vary widely in their mix of qualities. The fastest ones are extremely light but fragile and expensive. Most fill the middle ground between heavy poly and light composite construction; they're moderate in weight, cost, and durability.

Shortboards

Shortboards generally have less volume than longboards. Most have less than 140 liters, whereas longboards have more than 145 liters. More important, shortboards, unlike longboards, are designed for use in planing conditions, either primarily or exclusively. In short, if there isn't enough wind for you to plane (over 12 or 15 mph), you don't want to be on a shortboard. This makes shortboards very limited in their usefulness and suitability for the average novice.

Choosing the Proper Rig

A rig includes mast, boom, and universal joint, but the most important element is the sail. Sails, like boards, are specialized. Other than the basic light-wind sail that comes with an inexpensive board, there are race sails, wave sails, and slalom sails. Although I won't go into vast detail in explaining all the differences between the various types of sails, I will provide an overview of sails and other rig components.

Sails

Sails come in all different sizes: big ones for big people or light winds, small ones for light people or high winds. A big sail might be 10 square meters (110 square feet) in area, or about as big as the floor of a small bedroom. A small sail might be 2 square meters in area, the size of a big desk. Most often, windsurfers use sails between 5 and 8 square meters in size, and no matter where they live they use the metric system when talking about sail size. A sail of 6 square meters is usually called a "six-oh," a 6.5 is called a "six-five," and so on.

A light-wind sail works well in any situation where you're lightly powered. For example, when you're sailing in a 5-mph wind on a 5-square-meter sail, you're lightly powered. If the wind should increase to 12 mph, a smaller sail, say a 3-meter, will allow you to remain lightly powered.

Being "lightly powered" means not having to lean very hard against the pull of the sail. It results in being able to cruise at 3, 5, maybe 7 mph, but not being able to plane off at 20 or 30 mph. It means that the sail sustains minimal loading and thus does not have to be very rigid or stable. For as long as you sail only in lightly powered conditions, a light-wind sail will work fine for you.

However, when you begin to sail in more fully powered conditions and start to lean hard against a sail and load it with your body weight, a light-wind sail will no longer work well. Moderately powered and overpowered circumstances will make such a sail hard to handle and slow. To overcome this problem, sailmakers have designed sails that are rigid and stable enough to handle the high loads of powered windsurfing. These are called race, slalom, and wave sails. The race and slalom sails are best left to more advanced windsurfers, but a good wave sail, especially one with short battens, can work for either a pro or a novice.

Masts

The mast is the point at which a sailmaker begins the design process. Each sail is designed around a mast of a particular type, fitting a specific description. Thus the mast is as much a part of the sail as the cloth or the battens. This means that you should get exactly whatever mast is recommended for the sail that you buy. If you don't want or can't afford the specified mast for a particular sail, you should keep looking until you find a sail–mast combination that you want and can afford.

Masts are typically between 13 and 16 feet long and made of carbon fiber, aluminum, or fiberglass. Carbon fiber masts are the best for all windsurfers, even novices, because they are the lightest and easiest to lift out of the water. Not surprisingly, they're also the most expensive. Aluminum masts are an economical but heavier alternative to carbon. Fiberglass masts are the most durable and least costly, but they can weigh twice as much as a good carbon mast.

Booms

A typical boom consists of four main parts: the front end, the two main tubes, and the back end. The front end includes a clamp through which the boom can be attached to a mast, and the back end includes a length-adjustment mechanism through which the boom's length can be changed to fit sails of different size. The tubes are usually made of carbon fiber or aluminum—the former being stiffer, lighter, and more expensive than the latter.

The boom is an integral part of the rig, but it's not a part of the sail the way a mast is. Thus, the sail designer's specification of boom, if any, can be safely ignored. You can read about tests of specific booms in windsurfing magazines and decide exactly what combination of strength, stiffness, weight, ease of use, and cost you need. For now, though, you won't be placing big demands on your boom, so nearly any one will work.

Bases and Universal Joints

Many rigs include adjustable mast bases and heavy-duty universal joints. An adjustable base permits you to use different size sails on one mast by allowing you to extend the mast at the butt end. A durable universal joint allows you to sail in all conditions without concern about joint failure.

Because all bases and universals are adequate for the needs of nearly all windsurfers, the main point of concern is compatibility. A number of small

Types of Sails

There are four main types of sails, each ideally suited to a different kind of windsurfing.

Light-Wind Sails

If you sail in lightly powered conditions—either in very light winds or with very small sails—you can easily use a light-wind sail, which is the simplest and least costly sail available. It's made of inexpensive cloth, has few or no battens and no camber inducers, and is very easy to rig.

Wave Sails

Wave sails, like light-wind sails, are simple, light, and easy to rig, but they're also built to withstand very hard use. They work best in powered conditions, but many also work well when lightly powered.

Slalom Sails

A step up in complexity from the wave sail is the slalom sail, which, though not as light, handy, and easy to rig as a wave sail, has a stronger orientation toward speed. It's likely to have some camber inducers and a total of five or six battens, one or two of which will be very stiff.

Race Sails

The most complex, rigid, and stable sail is the race sail. A race sail can have many battens—seven is common—and camber inducers. These sails are heavy, relatively difficult to rig, and expensive— they are best left to experts.

parts are involved in the link between mast and board, and the parts from one manufacturer usually don't fit the parts from another. Expect, then, to choose a brand of base and universal that works with your board and mast and to stick with it. Don't try to mix and match parts from different manufacturers because chances are they won't match.

Choosing the Right Fin

The standard fins that come with most full-featured longboards, especially the expensive ones, are quite good. There's seldom a need to look for a better fin until you're well beyond the novice level. Then, when you get to the point that you're able to plane on your longboard, you need only make sure your fin is a "pointer" or "swept pointer" in the 45- to 60-square-inch range (typically 12 to 13 inches long). If you weigh between 150 and 170 pounds, you'll do well with a fin in the middle of that range.

The exception to this rule is when you sail in a place that has a lot of seaweed or kelp. If you do, you'll find that conventional fins collect seaweed the way a windshield collects bugs on a hot summer night (the main difference being that bugs don't stop the car in its tracks). The solution to this problem is a weed fin. Weed fins aren't as fast as conventional fins, but they're swept back at about a 45-degree angle so that the seaweed will slide off. A wide triangular-type weed fin is best for intermediates, whereas the narrower type will work for experts. Both types of weed fins can be used on shortboards, too.

Compatibility

One frustrating aspect of fin selection is that not all boards have the same kind of fin-attachment system, or "fin box." In fact, there are eight different kinds of fin boxes on the market, all but two of which are incompatible. A Mistral fin, for example, won't work on a BIC board, which won't accept a TIGA fin, which won't fit into a Seatrend board. Which fin box is best? The one used in BIC and Fanatic boards, called the Power Trim box, has the best combination of strength, versatility, and ease of use.

Construction

Fins are usually made of thermoplastics such as polycarbonate, molded fiberglass and carbon fiber, or hand-shaped fiberglass panels. Until you're an expert you need not be much concerned about fin construction.

What to Wear

The most basic windsurfing attire need be no more than a swimsuit, but there are many accessories that can improve safety and comfort.

Life Jackets and Footwear

The most important safety items are the life jacket and suitable footwear. In most countries windsurfing boards are considered to float well enough to be safe, so marine authorities don't require use of a life jacket or flotation device (PFD) when windsurfing. However, if you have any doubts at all about your swimming ability or your ability to handle the difficulties you may encounter on the water, be sure to wear a PFD.

Windsurfing is a remarkably safe sport, but you can never be too safe.

The one place a PFD should never be worn is the surf. That's because a key tactic for surviving in surf when separated from board and rig is to dive deep into the water, under breaking waves. A PFD disallows this and leaves the windsurfer entirely at the mercy of the surf. Of course only expert windsurfers should venture into surf at all.

Since you don't swim with shoes on, you may think there's no need to windsurf with them. Indeed, in the ideal location with the ideal equipment, footwear is probably unnecessary. Unfortunately, most of us sail from beaches that have sandspurs or worse and in waters that harbor hazards such as clam shells, sharp sticks, and so on. Therefore, tough, protective windsurfing booties or tennis shoes are highly recommended.

Lycra Suits, Sunscreen, and Sunglasses

Protection from the sun should be a major concern, especially if you're fair-skinned. In sunny or cloudy conditions, always protect your face with waterproof sunscreen that has a sun protection factor (SPF) rating of 15 or more and that guards against both types of ultraviolet radiation, UVA and UVB.

Studies have also shown that extended exposure to sunlight is correlated with high rates of eye cataracts. Sun, salt water, sand, and other irritants can also cause the growth of pterygia on the eye's corneas. For protection, wear high-quality, polarized sunglasses. Good sunglasses also reduce the glare from the water, make colors more vivid, and make it easier for you to see and interpret the ripples that wind makes on the water. Manufacturers of sunglasses such as Hobie, Bollé, and Oakley offer sport goggles that stay on your face even in strong winds and when you fall in the water.

If you want protection from the sun but don't like smearing your body with sunscreen, try a Lycra body suit. Lycra is a light, stretchy material that provides protection from the sun without inhibiting movement. A combination of very thin neoprene (or a similar material) and Lycra can help retain body warmth on a moderately warm day and still provide protection from the sun.

Wetsuits

At some point you may want to windsurf in cool weather or water. Even if the weather isn't cool, windsurfing in high winds can make you feel chilled, so some sort of neoprene wetsuit is called for. The most popular wetsuits are steamers, short-sleeved long johns, and shorties. The steamer, usually made of thick neoprene, is the warmest of the wetsuits and can keep you comfortably warm in near freezing conditions. Short-sleeved long johns are a good cool-weather option (air temperatures of 60 to 70 degrees Fahrenheit or 15 to 21 degrees Celsius) because they leave your arms free to move without encumbrance. Shorties are comfortable suits to wear just about anytime. They leave your arms and legs free to move, they're easy to put on and take off, and they conserve core body heat while leaving plenty of skin exposed for cooling.

An alternative to the wetsuit is the drysuit, which has watertight seals at the wrists, ankles, neck, and zipper. You can fall into ice-cold water wearing a drysuit without suffering the discomfort of freezing water trickling up your legs and down your back. Of course drysuits seldom prevent all water from coming in, and perspiration makes them a bit damp on the inside, no matter what. However, if you often sail in cold water, a drysuit is a good option.

Because much of your body heat is lost through your head, the part of the wetsuit that provides the most warmth for its size is the neoprene cap or hood. This is especially true when your hair is wet, the wind is strong, and the rest of your body is clad in neoprene.

CHOOSE THE RIGHT SUIT

Making the right choice about what wetsuit or drysuit to wear requires that you judge four key factors that determine how cold you are likely to get. Rate each of the following factors on a scale of 1 to 5, with 1 equaling mild conditions or low likelihood and 5 equaling hazardous conditions or strong likelihood. Then add up the points you've circled.

Air temperature	1	2	3	4	5
Water temperature	1	2	3	4	5
Wind strength	1	2	3	4	5
Chance of falling in the water	1	2	3	4	5

Total _____

Key: The higher the total score (i.e., the closer it is to 20), the warmer the suit should be.

People differ in their ability to generate body heat and tolerate cold, so no hard rules about wetsuit selection are possible. However, it's very important to remember that hypothermia—severe lowering of core body temperature—is a real danger on the water, even on seemingly warm days. Whenever you leave the beach, you should dress as if you might be out longer than you expect.

Gloves

Windsurfing can be hard on your hands. In cool weather your hands can get numb, and no matter what the conditions they can develop blisters. Some windsurfers turn to gloves for help.

Cold-weather gloves and mittens are usually thick and well insulated on the backhand side and thin or open on the palm side. The thick insulation protects the exposed back of the hand, while the thin or open part permits easy gripping of the boom. Some gloves are even prebent—they come from the factory with fingers already bent into a near fist—which makes gripping the boom easy.

The gloves most often used to keep hands from becoming blistered and callused are sailing gloves that conventional sailors use to protect their hands from rope burn and abrasion. They don't allow as good a grip on the boom as bare skin, though, so many windsurfers do without them.

Harness

A harness is a sort of sling that you can wear like shorts, a cummerbund, or a vest, depending on what type you have. It has a hook on the front that allows you to hang from lines affixed to the boom. Hanging from these lines—"hooking in," as we say—allows you to take the load off your arms. When you're first learning to sail with a harness, you should use a chest harness for ease of use.

Helmet

Twenty years ago, helmets on windsurfers were very rare. Now many windsurfers who go out in high winds and rough water have taken to wearing them. More and more relatively inexperienced windsurfers are enjoying the challenge of very rough conditions and have the good sense to take precautions. Professional windsurfers who have developed the reflexes necessary to avoid head injury seldom use helmets because they interfere with their ability to sense the wind, but less expert windsurfers have to be concerned about the mast or board striking them in the head.

Where to Get Equipment

If you've never windsurfed and you're thinking of borrowing a friend's equipment, forget it. Borrowed equipment probably won't work for you. It's likely to be too small or too complex, too modern or too beat up, and it will likely frustrate your first windsurfing experience.

(a) A chest harness is worn like a vest and supports the entire back. (b) A waist harness is the easiest to put on, the least restrictive, and the least supportive. (c) A seat harness is best for advanced slalom sailors and racers.

Instead, rent a board as part of the lesson package of a reputable windsurfing school, or buy something inexpensive like a used longboard or a kneesurfer. The rental option is especially attractive if you can combine it with a trip to a windsurfing resort. Resorts have the best gear, the most highly experienced instructors, and the best weather. They permit you to

AT A GLANCE: EQUIPMENT NEEDS

	Knee-surfer	Long-board	Short-board	4m sail	5m sail	6m sail	7m sail	8m sail	Mast	Boom	Wet-suit	Harness
Beginner /casual windsurfer	X											
Casual longboard sailor		X				X			X	X		X
Family	X	X				X			X	X		X
Recreational longboard racer or Olympic contender		X					X		X	X	X	X

	Knee-surfer	Long-board	Short-board	4m sail	5m sail	6m sail	7m sail	8m sail	Mast	Boom	Wet-suit	Harness
Dedicated high-wind slalom sailor			X	X	X	X			X	X	X	X
Dedicated high-wind wave sailor			X	X	X	X			X	X	X	X
Dedicated all-weather sailor		X	X	X	X	X	X	X	2	2	2	X
World Cup pro			10	3	4	4	3	1	15	15	3	2

AT A GLANCE: EQUIPMENT COSTS

Equipment	Cost (in U.S. dollars)
Kneesurfer with rig	$200–$300
Poly longboard without rig	$500–$650
Composite longboard	$700–$2,300
Poly shortboard	$300–$1,000
Composite shortboard	$700–$1,400
Basic 4- or 5-square-meter sail	$100–$150
Recreational longboard or slalom sail	$200–$500
Race sail	$400–$800
Fiberglass and epoxy mast	$70–$140
Aluminum mast	$150–$240
Carbon mast	$280–$400
Aluminum boom	$100–$250
Carbon boom	$280–$400
Fiberglass fin	$50–$150
Racing fin	$75–$225
Steamer wetsuit	$150–$300
Drysuit	$200–$400
Shorty wetsuit	$100–$150
Harness	$50–$100

spend some time on equipment and find out whether it works for you, so that when the time comes to make a purchase you can do so with confidence.

Once you have the knack of windsurfing and know that you want to get more involved, it will be time to look more seriously into buying your own gear. Your best source for personalized advice on windsurfing gear, technique, and just about everything else related to the sport is a good windsurfing specialty shop. A good shop has a proprietor or salesperson who is highly knowledgeable and who will let you try before you buy—someone with whom you can build rapport. The intricacies of windsurfing are such that this kind of relationship can enormously increase your understanding and enjoyment of the sport. How do you know if a shop has knowledgeable people? Talk to some of the shop's existing customers, preferably experienced windsurfers, and find out whether they're satisfied with the products and services offered.

Other buying opportunities, usually sponsored by good windsurfing shops, are swap meets. These offer a great chance for you to pick up good used gear at low prices, comparison shop conveniently, and take advantage of the expertise of shop personnel. Swap meets are also chances to meet other windsurfers from your area, talk about what equipment works for them, and learn where the good places to sail are.

Unfortunately, you can't find good shops in every town. They tend to cluster in windsurfing resorts and metropolitan areas where windsurfers abound. If you don't live near a good shop, you may be better off buying from a mail-order operation instead. The best source of information about mail-order options is other windsurfers who have gone that route as well.

3

WINDSURFING CORRECTLY

Although windsurfing is fundamentally no more difficult to master than snow skiing, the problem for novice windsurfers in the past has been they've had to learn the skills of a sailor and tightrope walker simultaneously. The intricacies of sailing are complex enough, but to learn them while balancing on a tippy, 2-foot-wide board is in many cases too much to ask. It's a sink-or-swim approach.

Thirty years ago the sport of snow skiing had a similar problem. Beginners were expected to learn how to careen down hills at 20 or 30 mph while also learning how to turn skis 7 feet long. Those long skis were difficult to turn, they were awkward, and they broke a lot of legs. As a result, skiing gained a reputation as a difficult, dangerous sport. Then came innovations like quick-release bindings and the Graduated Length Method of instruction where beginners were given relatively safe, easy-to-turn short skis. Suddenly, skiing became easy and even novices were able to enjoy the unique sensations, scenery, and ambiance of the skiing experience.

Windsurfing is undergoing a similar evolution today. Prospective windsurfers no longer have to take the old sink-or-swim approach. Big longboards, with more flotation and stability than ever, are now available at windsurfing schools, and a new type of board, the kneesurfer, allows you to master windsurfing's sailing skills in a stable kneeling position. This latter approach is promising because once you know how to handle the sail while kneeling, you can more easily go on to master the balancing skills of stand-up windsurfing.

In any case, whether you start on an extra-big board or on a kneesurfer, windsurfing is now easier to learn than ever before.

SAFETY TIP   Use the buddy system. Sailing with others is safer and more fun than sailing alone, so always sail with a buddy.

Learning to Use the Wind

As a windsurfer, your number one concern is the wind. Just as snow skiers always know which way is uphill, which way is downhill, and how steep the hill is, windsurfers always know which way is upwind (where the wind is coming from), which way is downwind (the direction the wind is blowing), and approximately how strong the wind is.

You determine wind direction and strength by looking at flags, watching how other boats and boards are sailing, feeling the wind on your face, neck, and scalp, and, most important, observing the ripples created by wind on the water. Wherever the wind is blowing hardest, the water has more ripples on it. Those ripples make the surface of the water look darker. Thus, you can see a gust of wind before it gets to you by watching for dark patches of water.

Awareness of the wind is such an important part of successful windsurfing that you should practice judging the wind at all times, even when you're not on the water. Wind that is not very strong, 0 to 10 mph (0 to 16 kph), is called "light wind." The appearance of the water when the wind is light varies from glass-like, to lightly rippled, to slightly "capping." This last term refers to "whitecaps," which are the white tops of wind-driven waves. Whitecaps become much larger and more numerous in "moderate winds"—11 to 20 mph (17 to 32 kph). When the wind is really strong—21 mph (33 kph) and up—we say we have "high winds." In high-wind conditions, the water is white-capping heavily.

The wind changes constantly. It increases and decreases (gusts and lulls) from moment to moment and from hour to hour. Wind that is light and pleasant at noon can rise to storm levels by midafternoon. That's why you must develop the habit of constantly monitoring the wind. Failure to do so makes windsurfing more difficult and less fun.

**SAFETY
TIP**

Learn to windsurf only in the lightest breezes. If you see whitecaps on the water, the wind is definitely too strong.

Finding a Good Sailing Site

It's not always possible to find ideal circumstances (wind, location, temperature, etc.) in which to learn to windsurf. As much as possible, though, you should seek out warm, light wind, and warm, smooth water. If the air temperature is less than 70 degrees Fahrenheit (21 degrees Celsius) and the water temperature under 60 degrees Fahrenheit (15 degrees Celsius), you should wear some sort of wetsuit.

Most important, don't go windsurfing in offshore wind—wind blowing from land to water—if the opposite shore is more than a few hundred yards away. That's because an offshore wind can blow you downwind—and beginners always end up downwind—away from the beach. On the other hand, an onshore or sideshore wind (wind blowing onto or parallel with the beach) will help keep you from drifting too far from shore.

Other more obvious hazards to avoid are rough water, ocean surf, and fast-flowing currents in rivers and ocean inlets. They can all be dangerous (see chapter 4). Seek advice from local sailors or fishers when you aren't sure whether a sailing site is safe.

How to Launch

Once you've found a good spot for windsurfing, you have to get your board and sail assembled, or "rigged," and to the water. All boards and sails come with their own brand-specific rigging instructions, so we needn't go over that here. Getting to the water, though, is another matter. The main thing you have to be concerned about is the wind catching the rig and pulling it from your grasp or knocking you over. To avoid this problem, always keep the side of the rig that has the mast in it upwind and keep at least one hand on the mast. When the wind catches it, you can simply let the rig "weathervane," align harmlessly with the wind. It's like holding a delta-wing kite by the nose rather than the tail.

Once the board and rig are in the water, you need only attach them and you're ready.

When carrying the rig, always make sure the mast is to the upwind side of the sail.

SAFETY TIP   Don't rig near overhead power lines. If your mast should come in contact with one, the result could be fatal.

How Windsurfing Works

A sail is like a wing. When it's held at the correct angle to the wind it generates a force called "lift" that works in a horizontal direction and powers the board across the water. If the sail is held at too small an angle to the wind, it acts more like a flag than a wing and generates no lift. When held at too great an angle, the sail acts like a stalled wing. It produces lift, but not as much as possible. When held at just the right angle, the sail produces the greatest possible amount of lift.

A centerboard (or fin) is also like a wing that generates force in a horizontal direction. It is the interaction of centerboard and sail that permits boards to go in directions other than straight downwind. Exactly how this interaction works is hard to visualize, but if you're familiar with the way a water skier cuts across the wake of a powerboat, and if you can imagine that the ski is like the fin of a board and the tow rope like the pull of the sail, then you can see how a windsurfer can travel perpendicular to the wind rather than just with it.

This interaction of the sail and centerboard even allows you to windsurf in an upwind direction. You can't go straight upwind, however—you have to zigzag. It's like taking a switchback trail up a steep hill.

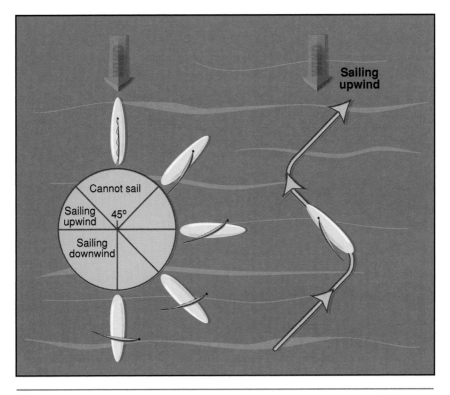

A board can travel on several different points of sail (or angles) to the wind. Sailing requires a zigzag, switchback-like course.

Of course, if you want to zigzag, you have to be able to turn. How do you do that? When you're windsurfing in a straight line the lateral forces from the sail and fin are in perfect balance. To turn, you simply have to upset this perfect balance. Steering, then, is simply a matter of tilting the sail. Tilting the sail to the front of the board or the back causes the board to turn downwind or upwind, respectively. Tilting the sail continuously in one direction and walking around the mast in the other causes the board to turn in circles.

BOARD ADJUSTMENTS

Most bicycles come with multiple gears that have to be adjusted depending on the terrain and whether the bike is traveling uphill, downhill, or on the level. Likewise, longboards come with mast track and centerboard, components that must be adjusted according to the strength of the wind and whether the board is sailing upwind, across the wind, or downwind.

The subtleties of adjusting centerboard and mast track are complex, but the most basic rule is this: When you're going slowly, the centerboard should be down and the mast forward; when you're going fast, the centerboard should be retracted and the mast at the back of the track. Centerboard and mast forward for low speed; centerboard and mast back for high speed. If you can keep in mind that fast jets usually have swept-back wings, you'll be able to remember this basic rule.

For now, you won't be going very fast, so you should have the centerboard down. The centerboard is down, so the mast foot should be forward. However, moving the mast all the way forward makes a board hard to turn, so it's best in the early stages of learning to keep the mast foot in the middle of the track.

Setting Sail

Once you've chosen a suitable sailing site and placed your equipment in the water, it's time to set sail. Don't try to jump up and take off immediately, however. No novice has ever done that successfully. Instead, take your time and follow these next instructions carefully.

CLIMB ABOARD

1. Stand in water 1 to 3 feet deep with the wind at your back and the board downwind of you. The centerline of the board should be perpendicular to the wind, and the sail should be lying in the water on the downwind side of the board.

2. Climb aboard and stand on the centerline straddling the mast foot. Holding the uphaul line as you stand up will help you maintain your balance.

3. Bend your knees, lean your body upwind, and slowly pull the sail out of the water. Don't try to jerk or muscle the sail up; let your body weight do the work. Most important, keep your back straight.

4. If you find that the sail is on the upwind side of the board, don't try to uphaul immediately. If you do, the wind will catch it and blow it in some unpredictable direction, most likely knocking you off the board in the process. Instead, pull the sail slightly out of the water and either drag it across an end of the board to the downwind side, or allow the wind to push on it and rotate you, the board, and the rig until the sail is on the downwind side. From this position you can uphaul normally.

5. Place your forward foot (the one nearer the front of the board) near the mast foot and point it toward the front of the board.

6. Place your back foot a bit more than shoulder width behind the front and point it across the board.

So far your sail has been flapping in the breeze like a flag. That's why you haven't been going anywhere. Now it's time to make the sail work like a wing and power you across the water.

1. Look in a direction perpendicular to the wind and find an easy-to-recognize landmark or a mark in the water. Be sure to pick a point that is not upwind or downwind, but across the wind. This will be your target. You'll aim for it and sail toward it.

2. Aim the board toward your target as you grasp the boom with your back hand—your back hand is the one nearer the tail of the board; your front hand is the one nearer the nose.

3. Let go of the mast, tilt it upwind slightly and toward the front of the board, and grasp the boom with your front hand.

4. Move your front hand away from your body while pulling your back hand toward your body. This action is called "sheeting in." It causes the sail to catch the wind and propel you forward.

5. When a gust of wind starts to pull you over, you can simply let go of the boom with your back hand (not the front hand). The sail will spill the wind and you'll be able to regain your balance and try again to sheet in.

6. To stop, drop the rig.

Once you catch the wind and start moving, you should concentrate on adopting a comfortable stance. Your front leg should be straight, your back leg slightly bent. Arms should be slightly, comfortably bent, with elbows down and hands about shoulder width apart. Most important, your body should be straight, not bent into a "C" curve. Your shoulders should be over your hips.

a   b

(a) Correct and (b) incorrect stance.

Adjusting the Sail

One of the hardest things about sailing is keeping the sail sheeted in properly at the best angle to the wind at all times. If the angle is too small, the sail spills the wind; it's like a flag and has no power. If the angle is too great, the sail stalls and has little power. The angle is correct when the front of the sail is almost fluttering but not quite. You learn to sense when the sail is at this angle by (a) spilling wind until the front of the sail starts to flutter (like a flag), then (b) pulling in with your back hand just enough to barely stop the flutter.

It's also tough to keep the board headed in the direction you want. The theory is simple: You just tilt the sail forward slightly when you want to go a little more downwind; you tilt backward to go upwind. In practice, however, it's easy to become confused and do the opposite. More difficult yet is keeping the sail angled properly to the wind *while* you're trying to steer. The only way to overcome these difficulties is to practice until proper angling of the sail and steering of the board become second nature.

PRACTICE TURNING —

1. To get a feel for how to turn and aim the board, tilt the sail toward the back of the board. It will turn so that the nose is aimed more upwind.

2. Tilt the sail toward the front of the board. The board will turn so that the nose is pointing more downwind.

3. If you want to turn completely around, continue tilting the sail in one direction as you walk to the other side of the board.

4. Now turn the board so that the centerline is perpendicular to the wind and the wind is at your back. This is the position to take when you're ready to start sailing.

Up, Down, Turn Around

You'll find that you tend to drift downwind while learning the basics. Therefore, you should work on sailing upwind almost from the start. Of course, you can't sail directly upwind; you have to zigzag. The ideal angle of your board to the wind is between 45 and 60 degrees.

How do you know if your board is at the right angle? The key is to develop an awareness of how fast you're going. If you're holding the sail at the correct angle to the wind—neither spilling nor stalling—but you have little or no speed, you're pointing the board too much upwind. To correct, tilt the sail forward slightly and head a little more across the wind. If, on the other hand, you have the sail angled correctly and your speed is good, you may not be headed upwind enough. Tilt the sail back slightly and head a bit more upwind. If your speed remains good even after you've headed upwind more, the new angle is better.

Sailing upwind is a constant process of changing the board's angle to the wind and monitoring the effect of such changes on your speed. Too slow means too much upwind; too fast means too much across the wind. Only practice can tell you what angle is just right.

Sailing downwind is easier than sailing upwind. You can just point your board straight downwind and go. No zigzagging, no switchbacks. You head downwind by tilting your sail forward. However, as the board heads more and more downwind, you tilt the sail more toward the upwind side of the board rather than toward the nose. Eventually, when you're headed straight downwind, the sail should be perpendicular to the centerline of the board and the mast should be to the side.

When you want to turn the board around and head the other way, you can perform a *tack* or a *jibe*. A tack involves heading in one direction across the wind, turning the board so that it's headed upwind, and continuing the turn until the board is headed across the wind in the opposite direction. A jibe is similar to a tack except that the board turns downwind rather than upwind.

MASTER THE TACK

1. Grasp the mast below the boom with your forward hand and steer the board upwind.

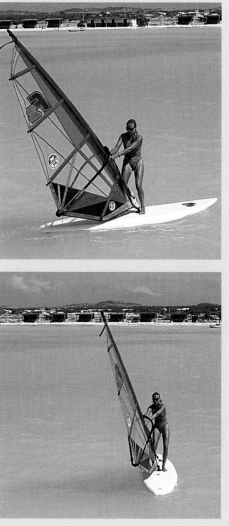

2. Keeping your front hand away from your body, adjust the angle of the sail to the wind as the board turns. Don't let the sail stall or spill wind as you continue turning.

3. When the bottom of the sail brushes against your back shin, step around the front of the mast with your forward foot. Release the boom with your back hand and step in front of the mast with your back foot.

4. Grasp the mast with your back hand and release with your front hand. Continue tilting the sail in the direction you want to go. You are now on the new tack.

5. Continue as if you had just uphauled the sail.

MASTER THE JIBE

1. Turn the board as if you are going to sail downwind.

2. Once headed downwind, tilt the rig to the side the mast is on. The board will turn in the direction away from the mast.

3. Release the boom from your back hand and grasp the mast.

4. Release the boom from your front hand.

5. Step to the other side of the board while you aim the board in the new direction across the wind.

6. Grasp the boom with both hands and continue sailing normally.

SAFETY TIP   Always stay with the board. It provides flotation and visibility. If you become separated from the rig, paddle the board to it. If you become separated from the board, swim to it immediately.

Powered Windsurfing

The time will come when you will venture out in more wind or with a bigger sail than you are accustomed to. In either case you will be moving toward what we call "powered" windsurfing. This is the type of windsurfing in which you have to use your body more aggressively to counter the force of the wind in the sail. It's the type that is no longer like flying a small kite and more like, well, flying a giant kite. The benefit is that you will start to skim across the water with the speed and freedom of a seagull.

You've already had a taste, perhaps, of the wind pulling the rig out of your hands. You may have resisted and been pulled over onto the rig. The bad news is that even if you'd had the strength of Hercules the same thing would have happened: You can't overpower the wind. The good news is that you don't need to. You need only to slow the wind down and change its direction slightly. In this way, windsurfing is much like one of those martial arts disciplines in which the master uses the strength of his opponent to his own advantage. When the opponent charges, the master steps deftly aside and redirects the opponent's head into a wall. When the wind howls and gusts, the skilled windsurfer calmly adjusts the sail, catches a bit less wind in it, and then accelerates to yet higher speeds.

This is not to say windsurfing requires no strength. Certainly, strength is a benefit, and you will have to use yours. But the importance of strength in recreational windsurfing is greatly exaggerated. There's no need to bulk up at the gym. You need mainly to know where and how to apply what strength you have.

Powered Stance

You may now be fully capable of sheeting in your sail in lightly powered conditions. However, powered conditions offer a whole new challenge, so your attempts to sheet in when powered may not be successful. You may find that every time you try to sheet in, the board turns stubbornly upwind, and you fall backward into the water. Then, if you overcome the first problem, you may find yourself being pulled over and onto the sail.

The stance you should strive for is to keep your arms straight, your feet on the upwind side of the board, your legs slightly bent, and your body leaning well upwind of the board.

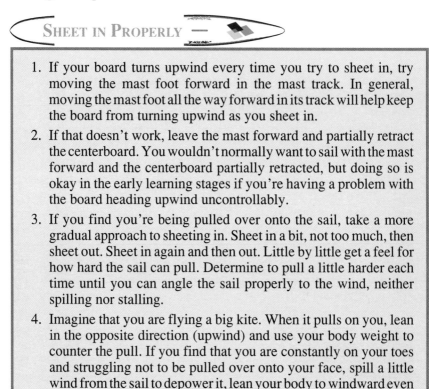

SHEET IN PROPERLY

1. If your board turns upwind every time you try to sheet in, try moving the mast foot forward in the mast track. In general, moving the mast foot all the way forward in its track will help keep the board from turning upwind as you sheet in.

2. If that doesn't work, leave the mast forward and partially retract the centerboard. You wouldn't normally want to sail with the mast forward and the centerboard partially retracted, but doing so is okay in the early learning stages if you're having a problem with the board heading upwind uncontrollably.

3. If you find you're being pulled over onto the sail, take a more gradual approach to sheeting in. Sheet in a bit, not too much, then sheet out. Sheet in again and then out. Little by little get a feel for how hard the sail can pull. Determine to pull a little harder each time until you can angle the sail properly to the wind, neither spilling nor stalling.

4. Imagine that you are flying a big kite. When it pulls on you, lean in the opposite direction (upwind) and use your body weight to counter the pull. If you find that you are constantly on your toes and struggling not to be pulled over onto your face, spill a little wind from the sail to depower it, lean your body to windward even more, and then sheet in fully again.

POSITION YOUR HANDS CORRECTLY

1. Hand position is not a big deal in lightly powered conditions. The more powered you are, however, the more precisely you have to place your hands. The correct distance between hands is no more than shoulder width.

2. Once you have your hands shoulder-width apart, note which arm has to do the most work when you're sailing. Most likely it'll be the back arm. If so, move your hands away from the mast a bit.

3. Keep sailing and adjusting your hand positions until the pull on each arm is, on average, equal.

Using a Harness

Powered sailing puts a much bigger load on your arms than lightly powered sailing does. It's a bit like hanging from a chin-up bar. Eventually your grip fails. A harness permits you to hang your weight from the boom with the help of metal and rope rather than just muscle and bone. Thus, your arms get a rest.

Exactly where your harness lines are attached to the boom is critically important. Placing them too far forward or back is like placing your hands incorrectly. If you're sailing with your hands correctly positioned, you need only place the harness line between your hands, with each end of the line next to a hand.

USE YOUR HARNESS CORRECTLY

1. Go out in very light wind and get the hang of swinging the harness line into, and dropping it out of, the harness hook.

2. Tug gently on the rig. This will set the harness lines swinging so that you need only position the hook to catch it.

3. Pushing down on the boom and lifting your torso allows the line to fall out of the hook. Practice these skills until they're automatic—only then should you use the harness in stronger winds.

4. When you do use the harness in strong winds, be aware that if you aren't able to unhook quickly, you can be violently thrown—catapulted, in fact—by the sail. Avoid catapults by unhooking at the first sign that you have lost control.

5. Take care not to be caught under the sail while hooked in. No one I know of has ever come to harm from this, but most harnesses have quick-release exit buckles just in case.

COMFORT TIP

Harness line length depends on your arm length. The general rule is that your arms should be nearly straight when you are hooked in and holding the boom. The easiest way to get this important dimension correct is to use adjustable-length harness lines.

Waterstarting

Wouldn't it be nice if after a fall from your board you could forego the part where you clamber back aboard and uphaul the sail? Wouldn't you rather just pop effortlessly back up to your feet, rig in hand, ready to continue sailing? Well, you can. In a maneuver called the *waterstart*, the sail pulls you out of the water rather than vice versa.

For the sail to pull you up, you'll need a moderate wind, or stronger, and the sail must be big enough to lift your weight. A 160-pound intermediate, for example, needs about a 6-square-meter sail and at least a 12-mph (19-kph) wind to waterstart successfully. An expert of the same weight can waterstart in less wind. A lighter person can manage with a smaller sail or less wind, whereas a heavier person will need a bigger sail or more wind.

LEARN THE BODY DIP

You begin to learn the basics of waterstarting by learning a trick called the *butt dip* and advancing to a full body dip.

1. Sail your longboard on a close reach.

2. Squat down, then stand back up.

3. Squat again, lower, and stand back up. You have to sheet out and depower the sail slightly as you dip down into the water, then sheet in and power up the sail to lift back up.

4. Try squatting lower and lower until you can dip your butt briefly into the water and then recover to the sailing position.

5. Go even further and dip your entire body in the water, sheet in, and lift back out to a sailing position. That's a waterstart.

Once you can do a body dip easily, you're ready for the harder part of waterstarting: getting started after an unplanned fall. This is more difficult because you have to get your rig, board, and body in the right positions, and you have to raise the sail clear of the water.

WATERSTART AFTER A FALL

1. The first step in a waterstart is to arrange the board and sail so that they are parallel with each other and perpendicular to the wind.

2. Make sure the sail is angled so that the mast is upwind of the clew.

3. Make sure the board and sail are aimed to go in the same direction. If necessary, turn the board around by dipping one end under the rig.

4. With one hand on the back of the board, use the other hand to grasp the mast a couple of feet above the boom. Lift the mast clear of the water by pulling it upwind and out of the water at the same time. If the rig is oriented properly to the wind, the wind will now blow under the rig and lift the back end of it clear of the water. If the back end of the sail remains stubbornly in the water, swim in an upwind direction and pull the rig, mast still out of the water, with you. This should allow the wind to lift the back of the sail clear of the water.

5. Now that the sail is clear, place both hands on the boom and handle the sail as if you were sailing in a standing position.

6. Place your feet on the board. Now you're in the familiar body dip position, so all you need to do is sheet in and lift out as if you were doing a simple body dip.

SAFETY TIP If you become overpowered during a waterstart, and the rig starts to pull you up before you're ready, simply spill some wind. If the rig starts to sink back toward the water, sheet in and power it up a bit.

Most experienced windsurfers view the waterstart as a shortboard sailing technique because it's most often used on shortboards. However, waterstarting can be done on nearly any board and is best learned on a longboard.

Align the mast with the board, mast on the upwind side of the sail.

Clear the sail from the water by lifting with one hand and pressing down on the back of the board with the other.

Using Footstraps

When you start sailing in fully powered conditions, and your board skims across the water on a fast plane, you'll find that keeping your feet from sliding across or bouncing off the board can be difficult. This is when you should start learning to use footstraps. You can slip your feet under the straps when you start to go fast, thereby maintaining firm contact between deck and sole.

Longboards are often equipped with four sets of footstraps (eight in all): One set on each side for sailing upwind—called "upwind" straps—and one set on each side for sailing on reaches—called "reaching" straps. Install the reaching straps according to the manufacturer's instructions. Leave the upwind straps off for now.

To use your footstraps you have to be powered up enough that you can sail in at least a semiplaning mode. For example, if you weigh 160 pounds, you should have 15-mph (24-kph) winds and a 5.5- or 6.0-square-meter sail.

If you're a novice to footstraps, you'll probably find that you can't get far enough back on the board to comfortably get your feet into the straps. Every time you try, the board turns upwind and you fall over backward. That's because you haven't learned to hang enough of your weight on the boom. Hanging on the boom transfers much of your body weight to the front of the board via the mast and thus helps steady the nose of the board and keep it tracking in the right direction. In fact, the whole trick to moving yourself back on the board, getting your feet into the straps, and sailing in full planing mode is hanging your weight on the boom via the harness. If you can't hang, you can't plane, and the better you hang, the faster you plane. It's that simple.

Once you're in the straps, you have to concentrate on your stance. Your arms and legs should be nearly straight, and you should be leaning over the water as much as you can. The more you can project your body out over the water upwind of the board and sail, the stronger and faster your sailing will be.

Planing well requires quite a bit of practice but not a lot of strength or effort. Balance is everything, and hanging your weight properly from the boom makes planing nearly as effortless as sitting on a porch swing.

COMFORT TIP

Adjust the straps so that when you put a foot in one you can see your entire big toe sticking out the other side. If you make the straps any smaller, your feet won't stay locked in when you need them to. If you make them any bigger, you may accidentally shove your foot so far into the strap that it becomes stuck at the wrong time.

GET INTO THE STRAPS

1. Hang from the boom by hooking into your harness line and bending your knees.

2. Put your front foot into the forward reaching strap.

3. Hang even more weight on the boom and put your back foot into the back strap.

Advanced and Expert Techniques

Once you can windsurf with a moderate amount of power in your sail and can perform basic maneuvers like the tack, jibe, and waterstart, you're ready to sail nearly any place a small sailboat can go. You're also ready to progress to a vast new world of advanced windsurfing techniques, such as taking advantage of windshifts, doing quicker tacks, jibing at high speed, and so on. The catalog of things to learn in windsurfing is huge and growing daily. Fortunately, many books and videos are available that can guide you in your next steps through this new territory.

4

WINDSURFING FITNESS AND SAFETY

You can windsurf in a pool

or a duck pond and if things don't go right you can just wade out. On the other hand, you can launch in the ocean, get caught in a storm, and spend hours (or even days) trying to get back to shore. Depending on where and how you do it, windsurfing can be as safe as taking a bath or as dangerous as bungee jumping with rubber bands.

All depends on your preparation. Along with knowing about windsurfing equipment and technique, you need to know how to prepare yourself physically for the sport and how to handle common physical problems that may arise. For safety's sake, you also need to know the basics about good windsurfing weather, how to rescue yourself when you misjudge the weather or break down, and how to deal with traffic on the water.

Serious windsurfing tends to develop lean and strong bodies, so one look at the average windsurfing professional suggests that windsurfing is a sport exclusively for highly trained athletes. This isn't so. Looking at professional windsurfers and deciding that average folks can't windsurf is like looking at Olympic-class 100-meter sprinters and concluding that most of us have no hope of running. The truth is, there's a whole range of levels at which windsurfing can be enjoyed, just as there's a range of speeds at which people can walk or run.

Windsurfing makes demands on your body only to the extent that you want it to. If you want light exercise, you can sail lightly powered. If you want a high-intensity workout, you can race or sail in waves. Either way, you get one of the most enjoyable workouts possible. Better yet, according to recent research, regular light workouts can provide the life-extending benefits formerly thought to result only from frequent high-intensity exercise. This means that activities like walking, cutting the grass, and low-intensity windsurfing, though they may not seem that demanding, are strenuous enough for the fitness needs of many people.

Are You Ready for Windsurfing?

Though lightly powered windsurfing may be no more strenuous than a walk in the park, it isn't quite the same thing. If you faint in the park, you're unlikely to drown. Risk is a part of windsurfing, as it is of every sport, so you should evaluate your physical condition and decide whether you want to take the risk inherent in the sport. Questions to consider are whether you have a condition that might cause you to lose consciousness without warning, whether you're likely to have a heart attack a half mile from land, whether your back is up to the task of uphauling a sail, and so on.

If you wonder if you're fit enough to take up windsurfing, get your doctor's opinion. If it turns out windsurfing is not an unreasonable risk for you, you're ready to learn more about the demands it is likely to make on your body and to prepare yourself gradually for the type of windsurfing you want to do.

Improving Your Windsurfing Fitness

How do you get in shape to windsurf? Actually, windsurfing is its own best exercise. If you start by sailing lightly powered and gradually work up to

PHYSICAL DEMANDS OF WINDSURFING

Lightly powered sailing: This is no more demanding than walking. It provides healthful, not strenuous, exercise.

Light-wind racing: This type of sailing involves pumping the sail—flapping it like a bird's wing. It requires good strength and very good aerobic fitness.

Wave sailing: This means jumping, surfing, turning around, and swimming after the board when a wave washes it away from you. All these activities require good all-around strength, flexibility, and aerobic fitness.

Slalom sailing: This kind of windsurfing can make moderate or exorbitant demands, depending on how aggressively you do it. If you sail fast in rough water, slalom sailing requires considerable strength and endurance, especially in the legs.

more demanding levels, your body will automatically become better fit for windsurfing. Here's how to make the first steps toward good windsurfing form.

Strength Conditioning

People look at windsurfing and think it must require a lot of upper-body strength. Leg strength, however, is what you should work on most.

Hiking up and down steep hills is one of the best exercises for developing the leg strength and endurance that windsurfing requires. A good workout includes at least 1,000 vertical feet of climbing (preferably 2,000) on an incline that's so steep you can't walk up it without resting occasionally. This sort of hike should take 1 to 2 hours and be repeated four to eight times a month. If a suitable hill isn't available, stairs also work well. If you don't live near hills or stairs, a stair machine is an acceptable alternative.

One problem with hiking steep hills is that it can be hard on the knees, especially going downhill. An alternative that's easier on the knees is mountain biking. On a multispeed bike you can keep the revolution rate of the pedals high enough that your knees are never highly loaded. Since you're coasting on the downhill sections, your knees don't have to endure a pounding.

Other exercises that help prepare you for windsurfing include crunches for the abdominal muscles; extensions for the lower back; all types of pull-ups for the latissimus dorsi; seated dips for the triceps; and tennis ball squeezes for the forearm muscles.

SAFETY TIP Don't perform strength exercises quickly. Take your time and move slowly and deliberately.

CRUNCHES

Crunches strengthen the front abdominal muscles, particularly the upper ones.

Lie on your back, bend your knees, and either cross your arms over your chest or clasp them behind your head. Slowly curl your torso until the middle of your back is just clear of the floor. Slowly lower your shoulders until they barely touch the floor, then repeat until you tire.

CRUNCHES

BACK EXTENSION

This exercise strengthens the lower back and the hamstring muscles of the thigh while placing little or no compression loads on the spine.

You can use apparatus designed specifically for this exercise or simply use a table with some padding on top. Lie on the table or apparatus with your hips resting on the edge and your legs under a restraining device (or have a partner hold your legs). Allow your torso to drop to a vertical position, head down. Clasp your hands behind your back or behind your head and slowly raise your torso to the horizontal position (don't arch your back). Hold for a moment, then slowly lower your torso to the vertical position again. Repeat.

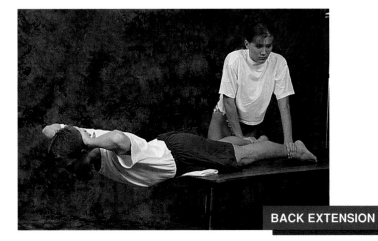

BACK EXTENSION

HORIZONTAL PULL-UPS There are several different ways to do pull-ups: vertical with hands close together, vertical with hands far apart, horizontal, and so on. The former work on the latissimus dorsi in general, and different variations concentrate loads on different areas. The latter are easier to perform and can work both the lats and upper back. Pull-ups also strengthen the biceps and forearms—important windsurfing muscles.

To perform the pull-up pictured, support a bar between two heavy chairs or tables and lie on the floor or ground with your chest under the bar. Grasp the bar and, keeping your body straight and heels on the floor, slowly pull your torso as close to the bar as you can. Hold for a moment and then lower your torso nearly to the floor. You can bend your legs and place your feet under your knees if performing the straight-leg version of this exercise is too difficult.

HORIZONTAL PULL-UPS

Aerobic Conditioning

The best aerobic exercise is walking. It's easy to do, easy on the feet and knees, and it provides an opportunity to relax and think. Stepping out for 30 or 40 minutes and walking 2 or 3 miles at least three times a week provides a reasonable minimum level of aerobic fitness.

Alternatives to light walking are biking, running, swimming, cross-country skiing, in-line skating, rowing, and so on. Using machines that simulate some of these activities is also effective. The more ambitious you are about your windsurfing, the more intense your aerobic workouts should be. The hiking that you may do to improve leg strength will also provide unparalleled aerobic conditioning.

Depending on your temperament and experience with exercise, you may be inclined to exert yourself too much or too little. The ideal is to push yourself only as much as you're comfortable with and no more. Start slowly and maintain any easy pace at first. As you warm up, you can increase the pace without discomfort. If you're breathing heavily but can carry on a conversation without gasping, you're maintaining a good pace.

If you're uncomfortable but feel guilty or ashamed when you slow down, slow down anyway. There's no shame in slowing down. Just don't quit. Go very slowly until your body tells you it's ready to speed up. Then stay well within your comfort range. The important thing is to exercise regularly, which means making each session a pleasant experience and never overdoing it. If you stay with your regular exercise program, you'll find eventually that you automatically want to go a little faster—and your improved fitness will allow you to.

A trick that may help you get started on your walk, run, or whatever is to tell yourself that you're going to take it easy, not push, just relax. That will get you going. Once you're going, you'll often feel like stepping up the pace a little more than you planned.

Stretching for Flexibility

Suppose you're well prepared and fit for the type of windsurfing you do. Do you still need to warm up before going on the water? Yes. No one can go from zero to 60 without a few minutes of revving. This is particularly true when you're sailing in cool weather. Run in place or do jumping jacks for a few minutes to get your blood flowing. Then stretch your back and hamstring muscles.

STANDING HAMSTRING STRETCH

This movement stretches the hamstring muscles at the backs of your thighs. Stretch both hamstrings at once by bending forward, or stretch each in turn, plus the muscles of the inner thigh, by bending to one side, as shown.

Stand with your legs almost double–shoulder-width apart and your knees slightly bent. Lean your torso down toward one leg as far as you comfortably can and hold for at least 20 seconds. Bend the other leg so as to stretch the inner thigh of the leg you're leaning toward. Repeat for the other leg.

STANDING HAMSTRING STRETCH

ANGRY CAT STRETCH

Standing on your hands and knees, lower your stomach toward the floor as much as possible by sagging your back. Then slowly raise your back into an arch. Contract your abdominal muscles as much as you can to arch your back as much as possible. Repeat slowly several times.

ANGRY CAT STRETCH

STANDING LAT AND TRICEPS STRETCH
Stand straight up and grasp your right wrist with your left hand. Pull your right arm to your head and arch your torso to the left. Continue arching and pulling while bending forward slightly at the waist and then straightening out. Continue for at least 20 seconds. Repeat on the other side, grasping your left wrist with your right hand and arching to the right.

STANDING LAT AND TRICEPS STRETCH

Cautions for Safe Windsurfing

Physical fitness helps you avoid the physical risks inherent in windsurfing and other sports, but it's no guarantee you won't encounter problems like hypothermia, back pain, sunburn, and dehydration. Be sure you know how to identify and deal with these problems.

Hypothermia

Hypothermia is a dangerous cooling of the body's core temperature caused by combinations of factors such as cold or cool air and water, high winds, and poor nutrition. Its onset is usually signaled by symptoms such as shivering, numbness, weakness, drowsiness, and poor mental function. You can prevent hypothermia by eating well, wearing a good wetsuit, and getting off the water at the first sign of shivering.

Children are especially susceptible to hypothermia because they have low body mass and lose heat quickly. To treat mild hypothermia, get into a warm place—a hot bath is ideal—and drink warm beverages. Stay away from alcohol. Severe hypothermia warrants immediate professional medical attention.

Back Pain

Since windsurfing is a no-impact sport with moderate strength requirements at most levels, it is generally good for your back. It strengthens abdominal and back muscles and improves flexibility. The stance that a good windsurfer takes when sailing without a harness involves hanging the body from the boom, stretching the spine rather than compressing it. An incorrect stance, however, can strain the back. If you're having trouble maintaining a correct stance, you're likely trying to sail with too much power—too big a sail or too much wind—before you're ready.

Even if your stance is good, you may find that a seat harness causes you back pain. If so, try a chest harness.

Sunburn

We've all experienced sunburn. It's not immediately life threatening but may have severe long-term consequences in the form of skin cancer. You avoid sunburn, of course, by dressing properly and using sunscreen. When you slip and get burned, however, treat the condition by drinking cool beverages (not alcohol), covering the burned area with burn ointment and cool, wet compresses, and taking aspirin or some similar pain reliever.

Dehydration

Dehydration, the excessive loss of bodily fluids and electrolytes stemming from inadequate intake of fluids, can result in severe conditions such as heat stroke. You can become dehydrated even in cold weather, particularly if you're sweating inside a hot drysuit. As with hypothermia, children are especially susceptible to dehydration.

Prevent dehydration by drinking plenty of fluids—cool water and sport drinks are good—*before* you feel thirsty. Treat dehydration by resting and drinking cool water, which gets into your system faster. Again, stay away from alcohol.

Wildlife

Encountering the fish, birds, and other living creatures in and around the oceans, lakes, and rivers is a part of the fun of windsurfing. On rare occasions, however, such encounters are troubling. Stepping from your board onto a clam can result in a nasty cut if you're not wearing shoes or booties; stepping on a stingray can be painful with or without footwear. Other risks are posed by jellyfish, Portuguese man-o-wars, sea urchins, and coral. The much-feared shark, however, is seldom seen; only a couple instances of shark attacks on windsurfers have been recorded in the 25 years of the sport's history.

We've touched upon some of the major risks involved in windsurfing. Keep in mind, though, that different sailing areas pose different risks, so you'll have to learn about the risks endemic to your particular sailing area and how to avoid them. It's also wise to know first aid.

Wind and Water

Environmental awareness is all the rage these days. It seems everyone is eager to use resources efficiently—minimal packaging on products, fuel-efficient vehicles, and so on. This sort of concern is nothing new for sailors, though. Since they've always had a 100% natural source of power, one that is highly limited and variable, they've had to be keenly aware of their environment and make the most of what it offered them.

Sailors have always had to understand weather patterns and sea currents, the effects of the sun and moon, and the locations of the stars. They've been concerned with the motions of waves, the dynamics of air and water flow, and the habits of various sea birds and creatures. Failure to be aware of the environment, to properly understand and use the wind, waves, and currents—in other words, failure to use resources efficiently—meant hardship or even death to the sailor.

The stakes for windsurfers are a bit lower than they were for Magellan. It's rare for a windsurfer to experience a truly life-threatening situation. However, mastery of windsurfing still requires knowledge of the sailing environment—an understanding of wind and water.

Wind

The force that wind exerts on a sail is proportional to the square of its velocity. This means that a 10-mph wind is 4 times more powerful than a 5-mph wind; a 20-mph wind is 16 times more powerful. That's why the wind can quickly become overpowering and why you have to respect it.

Wind is a big subject, of course, so you might want to find a book or two on wind and weather for sailors (see the appendix) and bone up on the subject as you improve your other windsurfing skills and knowledge.

Waves

Waves are created by the wind acting on the water. Small, irregular waves created by the local wind are called *chop*. Choppy waves are what most windsurfers sail in most of the time. They provide a third dimension to windsurfing and have often been compared with the "moguls" that snow skiers encounter. Chop helps make windsurfing exciting and poses no hazard. It can make learning difficult, though, so novice windsurfers should sail in water with chop less than 6 inches high.

The main thing to keep in mind about waves is that you should be at least an advanced windsurfer before you sail in rough water. Only experts should venture into breaking waves that are more than knee high. For more about waves, see books on sailing, surfing, and weather.

Current

Current is the least obvious force working on windsurfers. Unlike waves, current is not easy to see; unlike wind, it's not easy to feel. Still, it's always there to some extent, and it can be incredibly powerful.

To avoid problems caused by undetected current, make sure you know what currents prevail in the waters where you sail. Local fishermen, other windsurfers, and charts are good sources of information about currents.

In addition, when you're on the water, monitor the current frequently by sailing near a buoy or other fixed object and seeing whether the water is flowing past it. Another approach is to observe changes in the alignment of objects on shore. In any case, try to be aware of what current is prevailing and where it might take you should you break down or the wind die.

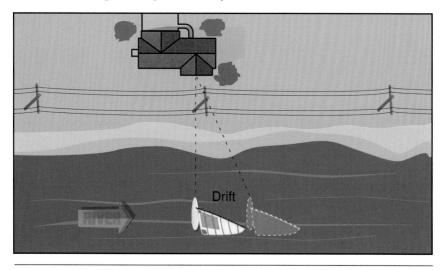

Watch two objects on land to determine whether you are drifting rapidly.

Weather and Tide Information

The mass-market weather forecasts you hear on the radio, watch on TV, and read in the newspaper are useful if you're an experienced and weather-conscious windsurfer. The forecast of an approaching cold front, for example, tells you that there may be good wind coming. However, no matter how much experience you have, you can't know for sure what the weather is like at various windsurfing beaches. Weather is highly localized, especially near mountains and coastlines, so skies can easily be cloudy and calm in one place and sunny and breezy just a few miles away. To overcome the problem of predicting what the weather will be like where, you can subscribe to a wind-reporting service. These services offer wind reports from anemometers located at the most popular windsurfing beaches and inform you of the latest windsurfing-specific weather forecasts (see the appendix for sources).

Emergency Rescue Skills

In the early days of windsurfing, whenever a windsurfer fell in the water some onlooker would immediately phone the Coast Guard with the urgent news that a boat had capsized. In the meantime, the windsurfer would get up and sail away, unconcerned. There may come a time, however, when the wind becomes too light or too strong or when some key part of your equipment fails and you find yourself unable to sail back to shore. If you're sailing with a buddy, as you should be, he or she will be able to help. In some situations, however, you may need to know how to rescue yourself.

SAFETY TIP Don't go anywhere you aren't prepared to rescue yourself from. Never expect anyone else to help you. Someone may help, but you can never be sure.

Assess the Situation

The first thing to do in any emergency is to calmly assess the situation. Consider factors such as wind strength and direction; where the wind is likely to push you; current strength and direction; where it will take you; the distance to your launch site; which shore you are most likely to fetch up on; whether there are any alternative safe havens such as sandbars, boats, or buoys nearby; and air and water temperature.

If after assessing the situation, self-rescue seems impossible, simply use your sail as a sea anchor to slow your rate of drift and sit quietly on the board to conserve energy. Use the international distress signal to communicate with passing boats.

Signal for help by waving your arms up and down to the side of and over your head.

Paddling to Safety

In almost every emergency, self-rescue is possible. After assessing the situation, you need to select the option that gets you back to land with the least effort. The possibilities are endless, but the most common involve paddling to the nearest attainable land.

I say nearest *attainable* land because the nearest land is not always attainable. If it's upwind or upcurrent, you could expend a great deal of energy paddling against the wind or current and not make any headway. It's far better to paddle across the wind or, better yet, downwind, even if the distance to land is somewhat greater.

To paddle effectively, you need to get your rig out of the water. You can balance it on the tail of the board or derig and lie on it. If the situation is really serious, don't hesitate to discard (and sink) your entire rig and paddle just the board. After all, the rig can be replaced—you can't.

The simplest form of self-rescue involves paddling the board while the rig is assembled. Of course, this method works only in very light winds, but it's useful also for paddling out of a wind shadow (an area of no wind) to where the breeze is. The alternative is to derig the sail on the water. This is what you do when the wind is so strong that paddling rigged won't work.

PADDLE WITH YOUR SAIL RIGGED

1. Drop your sail to the water and leave it attached to the board at the mast step.

2. Pull laterally on the uphaul line so that you drag the rig onto the back of the board. Make sure that the mast will be on the upwind side of the board when you start paddling to shore.

3. Balance the boom on the back of the board so that the sail is nearly or entirely clear of the water.

4. Lie on your stomach on the front of the board, your legs on each side of the mast foot and your feet helping to balance the sail on the board.

5. Start paddling.

Paddle With Your Sail Derigged

1. Lower your centerboard so that it is out of the way and will help stabilize your board.
2. If your sail has a few short battens, remove them.
3. Release the outhaul and roll the sail up against the mast.
4. Fold the boom parallel with the mast and tie the outhaul and uphaul around the mast and sail so that the sail doesn't unroll.
5. Place the rig longwise on the board and lie down on it. Start paddling.

Note: If your sail has full-length battens, removing them may be too much trouble. In that case you have to remove the boom from the mast, remove the mast from the sail, and roll the sail up. You then put everything on your board and lie uncomfortably on it as you paddle to shore.

Hitching a Ride

If you're lucky, someone will rescue you with a boat. If you don't have far to go, you can stay on your board with the sail rigged while the boat tows you to shore. The easy way to do this is to have a passenger on the boat hold the top of your mast, using the mast as a tow bar and keeping the sail clear of the water.

SAFETY TIP During a rescue, stay clear of the rescue boat's propeller. Confirm with the skipper of the boat that the propeller is out of gear, and stay clear of it in any case.

On the other hand, if you're some distance from shore, you should derig and hand your rig components to someone on the boat. You also have these options: staying on the board and being towed in; riding in the boat and towing the board; or putting both yourself and the board in the boat. The bigger the boat, the harder this last option is to execute. Should you try it, make sure you get on the boat *before* the board. Putting the board in first is hazardous because you can accidentally end up in the water without the board to float you.

SAFETY TIP When in doubt, don't go out. If you're not sure the weather and water conditions are safe, don't take the chance.

Rules of the Road

There are no stoplights on the water, no pedestrian cross-walks, and no double yellow lines. Instead there are maritime regulations designed to promote safety on the water. These are what we call the "rules of the road."

Naturally, avoiding injury to people and damage to property are the goals of these rules. Even the smallest collision between boats or ships can be very dangerous and destructive. Collision between windsurfers, on the other hand, may or may not be a problem. Certainly, two kneesurfers bumping into each other at 4 mph is no hazard. It can even be part of a game. But the head-on collision of two slalom boards travelling at 35 mph can be a disaster. Likewise, a collision between a windsurfer and a powerboat can be fatal.

To avoid these hazards, be aware of what's around you at all times, look through your sail window before you jibe, and follow the rules of the road.

SAFETY TIP   There are some special rules for sailing in surf. Be sure to ask more experienced windsurfers about surf etiquette in your area.

RULES OF THE ROAD

Rule #1: Windsurfers must keep clear of swimmers, surfers, rowers, paddlers, and all other self-powered water users.

Rule #2: Sailboats usually have the right-of-way (rights, for short) over powerboats. However, commercial vessels of all types have rights over pleasure boats, and large boats in confining channels have rights over smaller boats. Moreover, in some countries windsurfers are not considered sailboats; they are classified as beach toys and as such have no rights. In other words, though you are likely to hear and read that windsurfers have rights over powerboats, this rule does not apply in all situations and, depending on where you sail, may not apply at all to you. It's best to keep clear of powerboats.

Rule #3: When two boards are on opposite tacks, the one on port tack must keep clear of the one on starboard. When you're windsurfing with your left hand nearer the mast, you're on port tack. When your right hand is nearer the mast, you're on starboard tack. So, if your right hand is nearer the mast, you have right-of-way.

Rule #4: When two boards on the same tack converge, the one farther upwind must keep clear.

Rule #5: Any board in the process of tacking or jibing must keep clear of boards not tacking or jibing. When two boards are tacking or jibing at the same time, the one to the right has right-of-way.

Rule #6: The overtaking board must keep clear. This rule applies no matter what type of boats are involved—whether a board is overtaking a board, a sailboat, or a powerboat.

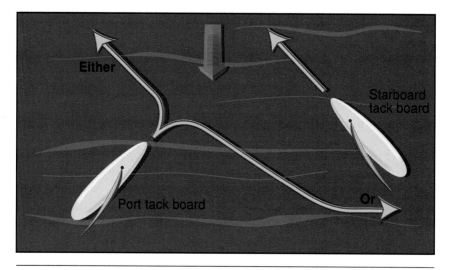

The board on port tack (left hand near the mast) must keep clear.

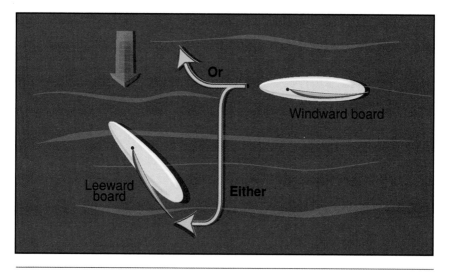

The board that is upwind, or to windward, of the other must keep clear.

 **SAFETY TIP** When in doubt, keep clear. If you're not sure you have right-of-way, stay well away from other water users.

5

THE BEST PLACES TO WINDSURF

When you consider that three-fourths of the earth is covered by water and that the wind blows at least a little almost every day, you realize there are more places to windsurf than there are to walk. How do you pick among them all? Your choice probably depends on what kind of windsurfing you like.

Do you prefer quiet days on a protected lake or the wind-whipped open seas of Hawaii? Do you like sailing with crowds of other windsurfers or with just a couple of close friends? Obviously, the best place for one person is not the best for another.

How do you know what kind of place is for you? The first step is to explore local spots, improve your skills, and get a better idea of what aspects of windsurfing you like the most. Then, peruse the descriptions of popular windsurfing areas presented in this chapter. You're sure to find some that suit your skills and temperament. The only thing left then is to get up and go.

Windsurfing Vacations

Just as ski resorts have sprung up in snowy mountains and hills, windsurfing resorts have been created on nearly every windy island and inlet around the world. Almost all the most popular places to windsurf sport at least a rental shop, and most offer lessons, accommodations, and nightlife.

Accommodations at a Caribbean windsurfing resort can cost as little as $200 per week, and equipment rental typically costs about $200 to $300 per week. Special "high-performance" equipment packages are often available for $500 or $600.

The staff members at resorts are usually helpful even if you don't need lessons. They rig the sails and maintain the equipment in good order. In some cases they even carry the equipment to the water's edge. They're always on the lookout for windsurfers in trouble and generally have a boat handy in case someone needs to be rescued.

Just as ski resorts have high and low seasons according to whether there's snow on the ground, windsurfing resorts have high and low seasons according to the wind and air temperature. In midlatitude climes, the wind is often strongest and most consistent in the winter, but the temperature is too cold for all but the most fanatical windsurfers. Thus, places like Lake Garda in Italy and the Columbia River Gorge in the U.S. have a spring-summer-fall season of about 5 months or less. Low-latitude resorts, such as those in the Caribbean and Hawaii, have warm weather year-round, but the winds are not always consistent. Hawaii, for example, has erratic winds and often rainy weather from December to early March but drier weather and spectacularly consistent winds in the spring, summer, and fall. Aruba, in the Caribbean, has rainy weather and inconsistent winds for a month or two in the fall, but that gives way to dry, windy weather that kicks in during December and remains through summer.

If for any reason you don't particularly want a lot of wind, you need not shy away from the windy season at windsurfing resorts. Most resorts experience high winds for only part of each day and at only some of their sailing areas. On the Island of Margarita in the southwestern Caribbean, for example, the wind is generally much lighter in the morning than in the afternoon. In the Columbia River Gorge, the wind is usually much lighter at the Hood River Marina than at the Hatchery less than 3 miles away. Thus, the high season at most resorts can accommodate any windsurfing taste, whether it runs to high winds or light, rough water or smooth.

Perhaps most important, if you have family that you would like to take on a windsurfing vacation, there are resorts that offer activities—both on and off the water—for every member. The Club Med in St. Lucia, for example, is highly regarded for its family offerings, and there are windsurfing schools in the Columbia River Gorge that offer instructional programs for children and teens.

Transporting Windsurfing Equipment

Before you can enjoy the best places to windsurf, you have to get to them. If the only board you own is a simple inflatable, you can throw it in the trunk of the car and be on your way. But most windsurfing gear is too bulky for such casual treatment, so traveling short distances will require you to have either a cargo van or roof racks for your car. If you're traveling by air, you'll need airline-proof protective gear bags.

Roof Racks

Roof racks used to be used by carpenters and painters for hauling odd bits of lumber and ladders. They were crude, stark, and cheap. Since the early 1980s, however, roof racks have undergone something of a revolution. At the demand of millions of bicyclers, paddlers, surfers, and windsurfers, rack manufacturers like Thule, Terzo, and Yakima have come out with slick, polished, sports-oriented roof racks. Today's racks will fit nearly any car—with rain gutters or without—and safely carry nearly any piece of sporting equipment that one person can lift.

When buying a rack you'll have to decide whether it should be soft or hard, whether it should lock onto the car, and whether you need the kind that doesn't require rain gutters on the car.

The ones that fit on rain gutters are best if you carry a lot of boards because gutters tend to be strong. The others can dent your car's roof or mar the paint if you don't use them carefully or if you load them too heavily. Still, if you don't have gutters, they're the only option.

An approach to carrying gear other than boards is a cartop box. These fiberglass boxes, which typically cost between $300 and $500, can carry booms, sails, masts, and other accessories. They can be locked shut and locked to the top of the car, and they have a streamlined shape that helps improve gas mileage.

SOFT VERSUS HARD RACKS

Soft racks	Inexpensive ($30 to $40)
	Fabric straps and plastic foam
	Very easy to remove from roof
	Compact and easy to store in glove box
	Low carrying capacity (one board)
	Don't lock onto roof
Hard racks	Expensive ($100 and up)
	Steel and aluminum
	Harder to remove from roof
	Bulky
	High capacity (several boards)
	Can lock onto roof

Airlines

If your destination is out of driving range, you can usually take your gear on flights as excess baggage. Just as most airlines allow golfers to take clubs and skiers to take skis, they'll let you take your windsurfing equipment. It's best to make it easy for them, though. Your board should be in a well-padded travel bag, such as those produced by Da Kine, Visual Speed, Lakes Bay, and others. Travel bags feature a minimum of a half inch of plastic foam such as ethafoam on all sides and usually cost between $200 and $350. If your board is light and fragile, wrap a layer of bubble wrap (available at packaging suppliers) around it before putting it into the bag.

If you're not taking much gear—a board, boom, mast, and one or two sails—you can fit everything in a big board bag. Just be sure to pad the board against damage from the boom. The total weight will run about 60 pounds, but that's manageable. If you're taking a bit more gear, try putting a board and a couple of booms in one bag and packing the sails and masts in a separate bag.

Most U.S. airlines define a "windsurfer" as three pieces of baggage—board, mast, and boom—and charge $75 to carry the lot. This practice is not followed worldwide, however, so charges vary enormously. To avoid unpleasant surprises at check-in, call your airline and ask the agent to enter a note on your record indicating (a) that you have been cleared to check in windsurfing equipment and (b) the excess baggage charge that you have been quoted.

Local Outings

Local windsurfing outings don't necessarily require much planning. If you live on a lake, you can pop out for a quick sail on the spur of the moment. However, if you have to travel to get to a launch site, or if you're planning to explore a new place, there are a couple of ways to prepare.

The first thing on any windsurfing checklist should be, "check the weather." The weather is a big concern before and during any windsurfing session for both convenience and safety reasons. Check the weather before you ever leave home, as there's no sense in driving to the beach if the wind is likely to be too light or too strong for the kind of windsurfing you plan to do. Also be alert for forecasts of lightning storms or other changes in the weather that could pose a threat.

Where available, your best source of weather information for your intended sailing site is one of the windsurfing-oriented wind-forecast services. A weather radio is the next best option.

If you want to explore new waters, buy a chart or map of the area you're planning to sail. A chart is a hydrographic or marine map of a body of water. It shows coasts, river banks, rocks, channels, harbors, bays, navigational markers, the orientation of these features with respect to the points of the compass, and water depths. Careful study will not only alert you to potential hazards in the area (e.g., strong currents or barely covered rocks) but may give you ideas about things to see and explore.

Of course there's no substitute for the knowledge and opinions of windsurfers familiar with a particular sailing site, so it's best to seek them out and ask their advice. The folks at windsurfing specialty shops are always willing and usually able to offer good advice. The sailing and windsurfing federations and associations of most countries maintain complete, up-to-date lists of local windsurfing clubs, so you can usually track down experienced, knowledgeable windsurfers in your area.

Windsurfing in the U.S.

America is a land of many lakes, rivers, bays, and coasts. There is such an abundance of great places to sail that no list could be complete. The most popular windsurfing places, however, tend to be those that are windiest, so these are the ones mentioned on this short list.

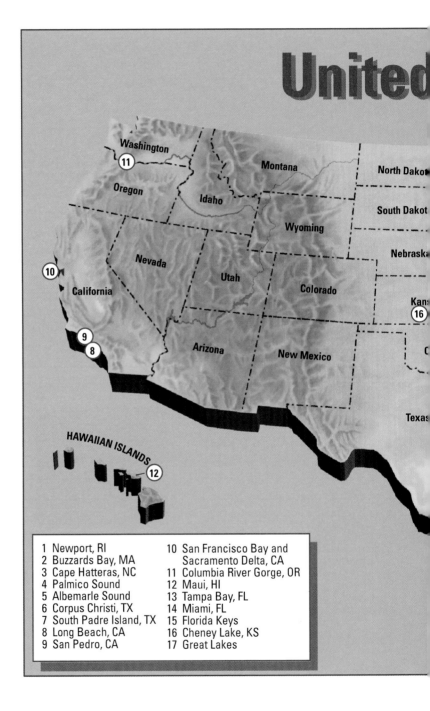

United

1 Newport, RI	10 San Francisco Bay and
2 Buzzards Bay, MA	Sacramento Delta, CA
3 Cape Hatteras, NC	11 Columbia River Gorge, OR
4 Palmico Sound	12 Maui, HI
5 Albemarle Sound	13 Tampa Bay, FL
6 Corpus Christi, TX	14 Miami, FL
7 South Padre Island, TX	15 Florida Keys
8 Long Beach, CA	16 Cheney Lake, KS
9 San Pedro, CA	17 Great Lakes

States

Minnesota

Wisconsin

Michigan

Iowa

Illinois Indiana Ohio

Missouri

'chita

Kentucky

Tennessee

Arkansas

Louisiana

Mississippi

New York

Pennsylvania

West
Virginia Virginia

North Carolina

South
Carolina

Georgia

Alabama

Maine

VT NH

Mass.

Conn. RI

NJ

MD Delaware

Florida

ATLANTIC OCEAN

N

Cape Hatteras

The entire east coast of the U.S. has an abundance of both water and wind. North of Long Island, New York, there is excellent windsurfing at Newport, Rhode Island, and in Buzzards Bay, south of Boston. From Long Island southward to Miami are barrier islands that protect shallow inland waters from the open Atlantic and help strengthen the summer sea breezes. In the middle of this abundance of great windsurfing sits Cape Hatteras, North Carolina.

Hatteras has been known for centuries as the graveyard of the Atlantic because of the many ships sunk by the violent, quick-forming storms that sweep past. And, of course, just 90 or so years ago the Wright brothers used the reliable, steady winds of Kill Devil Hills—a few miles north of Cape Hatteras—to help them learn to fly. Most recently, windsurfers have started trekking to Hatteras in droves, attracted by the same winds that brought the Wright brothers.

On the west side of the barrier islands that make up the Cape Hatteras area are shallow, brackish bays called Pamlico Sound and Albemarle Sound. These bays are so shallow that water is seldom more than chest deep, so they are safe and unintimidating places for windsurfers of all ability levels. On the east side of the outer banks is the Atlantic Ocean. The currents here can be strong and the waves huge, so only the most expert windsurfers venture out into the ocean. For those who can deal with it, the ocean off Hatteras offers some of the most challenging and satisfying jumping and surfing conditions on the east coast.

The lighthouse at Cape Hatteras is where the wave-sailing experts go when the wind is strong out of the northeast.

The best time of year for windsurfing Hatteras is the fall, September to late November, when the water is still warm, the air is not too cool yet, and the winds have shaken off their summer lethargy. The next best time is spring, April through June. The water is cooler in the spring, but sea breezes in the Kitty Hawk area (near Kill Devil Hills) are better than in the fall, and warm southerly winds can blow for days on end.

SOUTH TEXAS

Corpus Christi and South Padre Island, Texas, are popular refuges for windsurfers, particularly those who like to drive rather than fly to their winter and spring vacation spots. Both sites offer shallow inland waters protected from the Gulf of Mexico by Padre Island, as well as the rougher waters and surf of the gulf.

The city of Corpus Christi borders Corpus Christi Bay, which serves as the venue for the U.S. Open windsurfing regatta each year over Memorial Day weekend. The South Padre area offers the one-of-a-kind Brownsville Ship Channel—a canal from the gulf to the city of Brownsville—where the South Texas Speed Trials, a speedsailing competition, takes place every year around Easter.

The south Texas season extends from October to June, but December, January, and February can be quite chilly some years. The best combination of warm weather and wind kicks in sometime during March and extends through early June.

SAN FRANCISCO BAY AND SACRAMENTO DELTA

The west coast of the U.S. is much more rugged than the east coast. California, for example, has few sailing sites protected from the rough waters of the ocean. Still, in San Diego, there's Mission Bay, and in the Los Angeles area places like Long Beach and San Pedro, where the water is protected by the huge manmade breakwater that forms Los Angeles harbor. Summer winds in the Los Angeles area tend to be steady, reliable, and strong enough to satisfy the wind cravings of most windsurfers. On unprotected stretches of coast there are many excellent wave sailing spots. Inland, there are a few good windsurfing lakes.

The most popular places for windsurfing in California are the San Francisco Bay Area and the Sacramento Delta, just east of Oakland. The waters in the bay and delta are protected from the ocean swells and the chilly fog that hugs the northern California coast in the summer. Moreover, the large contrast in temperature between the cool ocean and hot Sacramento valley creates a strong, reliable sea breeze on most afternoons in the summer. The result is one of the few places in the world that a stockbroker

The Golden Gate Bridge makes a terrific backdrop for IMCO Olympic class racing.

or banker can regularly leave a downtown office at 5 o'clock to sail in 15- to 30-mph winds from 5:30 to 8.

Some of the most-used launches are Chrissy Field, near the Golden Gate Bridge; Berkeley Marina, on the east side of the bay; Coyote Point, to the south of San Francisco; and Sherman Island, near Rio Vista, east of Oakland.

Summer windsurfing weather usually starts showing up in Northern California sometime in March and lasts at least through August.

COLUMBIA RIVER GORGE

Far from the urban hurry of San Francisco, near the more relaxed city of Portland, Oregon, is the most popular summer windsurfing venue in North America: the Columbia River Gorge. Centered in the heart of the gorge is the small town of Hood River, home to dozens of windsurfing shops—more shops, in fact, than you'll find in any other city in the country. Why? The gorge has some of the strongest and most reliable summer winds in the world, so hoards of fanatical windsurfers descend on Hood River every year.

The appeal of the gorge is not limited to its winds, however. Fruit growers and loggers have prospered in the region for years, and outdoor sportsmen and women enjoy the area's outstanding hiking, biking, and river rafting. Nearby, Mount Hood offers the best summer skiing and snowboarding in the country. Recently designated a National Scenic Area, the gorge has something for everyone, especially windsurfers.

The gorge's westerly winds begin to blow regularly in April and continue through October. The water is quite cool early in the season—typically about 50 degrees Fahrenheit (10 degrees Celsius) in April—but it warms to the mid-60s (15 degrees Celsius) by midsummer, when the winds are most reliable and the weather warmest.

MAUI

Hawaii is the cathedral of windsurfing, the island of Maui is the nave, and the north shore of Maui is the altar. Windsurfers from around the world come to worship the wind on the north shore of Maui and to bathe in water made, to them, holy by the combination of warm, sunny weather, strong trade winds, and powerful ocean swells that break at just the right angle to the wind. There's simply no place known that's better than Maui for high-wind, high-excitement windsurfing.

If you're good enough, you can fly with the flying fish, sail with the whales, or blast across the 7-mile channel to the island of Molokai. On days when you're too tired to sail anymore, you can coast downhill for some 30 miles from the top of Haleakala, the 10,000-foot (3,000-meter) dormant volcano that forms the east portion of Maui.

Maui's trade winds blow fairly consistently from March through November, and they are most reliable from May to August. Meanwhile, the best waves roll in during the fall, winter, and spring, so pros and experts who want the best combination of wind and waves prefer Maui in the spring and fall. Every April and November, Maui's Ho'okipa Beach is the venue for major international windsurfing competitions.

OTHER U.S. DESTINATIONS

There are truly innumerable other places to windsurf. One of the windiest is Los Barrilles, near Cabo San Lucas at the southern tip of Baja, California (windiest December through February). Florida's Tampa Bay, Miami coast, and the Keys offer other exciting areas to windsurf. Even in the middle of North America, there are places like Cheney Lake in Kansas, where the locals say it isn't really windy 'til the cows blow over (best in the spring and fall); Salt Lake City, where a windsurfing lake is being built to take advantage of the area's good wind; Lake Mojave, just north of the Bullhead City (Arizona)-Laughlin (Nevada) area (best in spring and fall); and, of course, the Great Lakes.

In every case, however, the wind may or may not be your focus. Big wind days in windsurfing are like big powder days in snow skiing: You don't have to have powder to have fun skiing—unless you're incredibly spoiled—and you don't need big winds to have fun windsurfing.

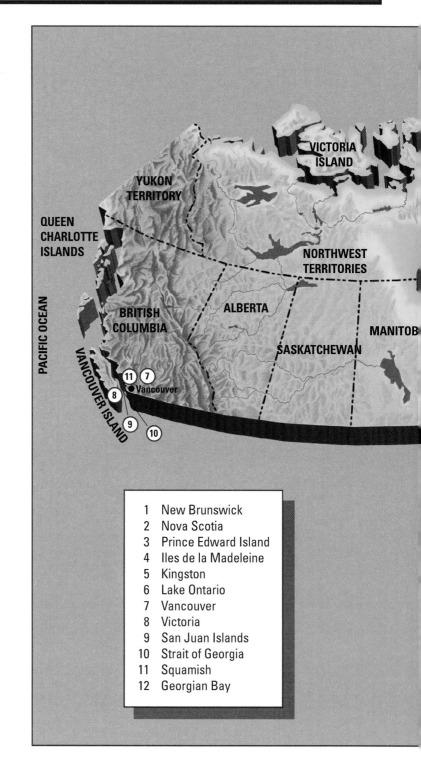

QUEEN
CHARLOTTE
ISLANDS

YUKON
TERRITORY

VICTORIA
ISLAND

NORTHWEST
TERRITORIES

PACIFIC OCEAN

VANCOUVER ISLAND

BRITISH
COLUMBIA

ALBERTA

SASKATCHEWAN

MANITOB

⑪ ⑦
⑧ ●Vancouver
⑨ ⑩

1 New Brunswick
2 Nova Scotia
3 Prince Edward Island
4 Iles de la Madeleine
5 Kingston
6 Lake Ontario
7 Vancouver
8 Victoria
9 San Juan Islands
10 Strait of Georgia
11 Squamish
12 Georgian Bay

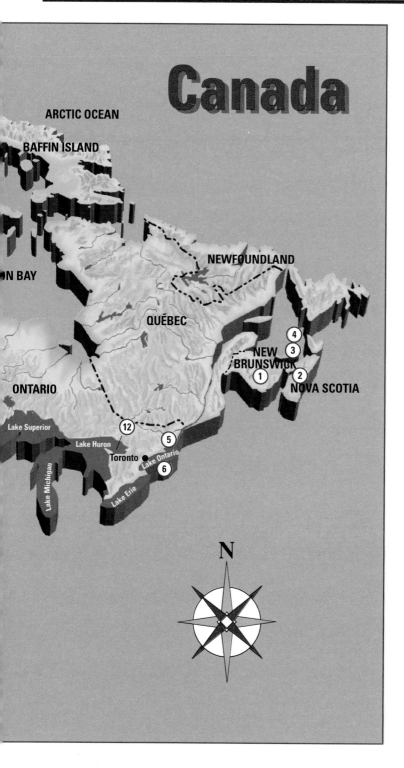

Canada

ARCTIC OCEAN

BAFFIN ISLAND

N BAY

NEWFOUNDLAND

QUÉBEC

NEW
BRUNSWICK

ONTARIO

NOVA SCOTIA

Lake Superior

Lake Huron

Toronto

Lake Ontario

Lake Michigan

Lake Erie

N

Windsurfing Canada

Though Canada has a short warm season and not as much hospitable coastline as its southern neighbor, the country has produced some of the world's top windsurfing sail and board designers, as well as some very competitive racers. These standouts had to learn somewhere, of course, and many got started at Canada's superb windsurfing destinations.

THE MARITIME PROVINCES

Canada's Maritimes, New Brunswick, Nova Scotia, and Prince Edward Island have numerous lakes and bays. Prince Edward Island is particularly noted as a summer windsurfing destination, partly because of its relaxed island atmosphere. Another appealing aspect of Prince Edward Island is that the water temperature of Northumberland Strait to the south of the island approaches the upper 60s Fahrenheit (15 degrees Celsius) in the summer. The best combination of wind and warm weather occurs here from late August to late September.

Just north of Prince Edward Island, in the Gulf of St. Lawrence, are the Iles de la Madeleine. These islands are small and sparsely inhabited, and they lie so low in the water that the wind can blow over them uninterrupted. Thus, the protected, flat-water, easy-sailing bays between the islands are swept by strong, steady winds. At the same time, the exposed beaches have surf and water rough enough to satisfy the most avid expert. The peak windsurfing season here is September also, and though the water is not as warm as it is south of Prince Edward Island, serious windsurfers prefer the conditions offered by the Iles de la Madeleine.

KINGSTON, ONTARIO

Georgian Bay, just north of Toronto, and the Great Lakes offer good windsurfing. One of the most popular of these areas is Kingston, at the northeast corner of Lake Ontario. Because Lake Ontario is deep, the water stays cool, even in the summer. The cool water working in tandem with the hot land on summer days creates a southwesterly sea breeze, which augments the prevailing southwesterly gradient wind and results in the best sailing for miles around in July and August.

BRITISH COLUMBIA

On Canada's west coast lie cities such as Vancouver and Victoria, the San Juan Islands, and bodies of water such as the Strait of Georgia and the Pacific Ocean. The Vancouver area doesn't have weather or water as warm in August as, say, Kingston, but neither does it have the extreme cold that eastern Canadians face in the winter. Consequently, the Vancouver area has

Although Canada is cold much of the year, many world-class windsurfing sail makers and competitors have come from there.

a sailing season that's surprisingly long for such a northern clime—April to October.

The most popular windsurfing site in western Canada is near the town of Squamish, at the north end of Howe Sound, an estuary that becomes less than a mile wide in the area where the windsurfers sail. The water is cold, but the wind is incredibly reliable, blowing between 12 and 25 mph (20 and 42 kph) most afternoons in the summer. Squamish offers a choice between somewhat protected water downwind of a berm that the windsurfers launch from and the exposed waters in the middle of the estuary. There's a lot of current here, and depending on the state of the tide, the water in the middle can be extremely choppy (during the ebb) or reasonably flat (during the flood).

The Caribbean

Windsurfing resorts throughout the Caribbean are favorites of windsurfers from both the Americas and Europe. Islands like Aruba, Barbados, Bonaire, the Dominican Republic, Grand Cayman, Margarita, Puerto Rico, St. Barts, and St. Lucia have consistent trade winds and some of the most beautiful waters in the world. Each boasts its own unique cultural flavor, from the "Little England" quality of Barbados to the "Little Holland" quality of Aruba.

These islands offer both protected flat-water conditions and open-ocean sailing. Some even have decent surf. Barbados, the Dominican Republic, and Puerto Rico, in particular, have good surf, while Aruba and Margarita are known for their extraordinary flat-water sites.

The trade winds throughout most of the Caribbean recover from their fall rainy season blahs and kick in consistently around Christmastime. They tend to be strongest in January through June—averaging a daily high of about 20 mph (33 kph)—then gradually wane through summer. The air temperature of course averages highs in the mid-80s Fahrenheit (27 degrees Celsius) year-round, while the water averages in the 70s (21 degrees Celsius).

Britannia Rules the Waves

Because England is an island, it's not surprising that most U.K. sailors have good windsurfing conditions a short drive away in any direction. The generally cool water and weather, though, and the roughness of the waters make windsurfing in the Atlantic, English Channel, and North Sea an affair primarily for advanced and expert windsurfers. Moreover, the fact that tidal variations are quite large means that currents can be very strong even where the water is seemingly calm and protected. Inland lakes and the upper reaches of protected estuaries, such as the Thames, are good for novices, but they are not the places found on many "best of" lists.

SOUTHWEST ENGLAND

The southwestern corner of England, the north Cornwall and Devon coast southwest of Bristol, is popular among wave-sailing experts because of its exposure to strong storm winds and waves from the westerly quadrant. Saunton Sands in Devon has a long sandy, gently shelving beach that's exposed to prevailing southwesterly winds. Farther to the southwest is Harlyn, a somewhat sheltered beach, and Newquay, a beach popular among surfers as well as windsurfers.

THE SOUTH COAST

According to Bill Dawes of *Boards* magazine, the south coast (between Bournemouth and Brighton) is the busiest part of the British windsurfing scene, in part because it's within an hour or so driving time from London. The two biggest sailing spots in this area are Hayling Island and Wittering, which are located on either side of Chichester Harbor. The Hayling Island site offers the sheltered, smooth waters of Chichester and Langston harbors and good sailing at mid to high tide; it is the best site on the south coast when

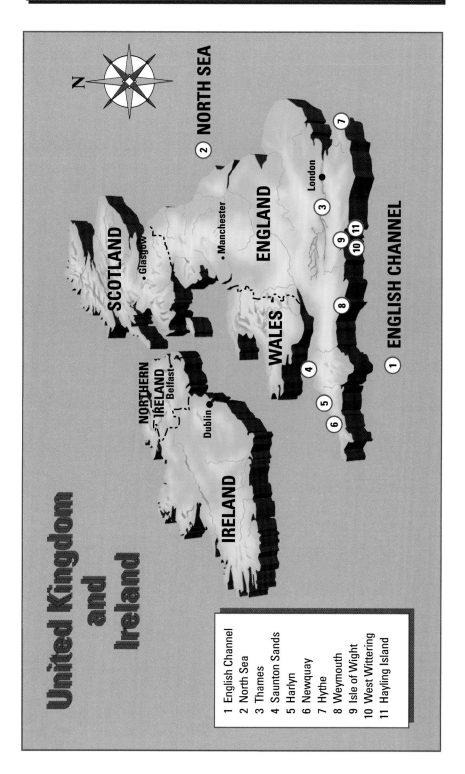

United Kingdom and Ireland

N

NORTH SEA

SCOTLAND
• Glasgow

NORTHERN IRELAND
Belfast

IRELAND
Dublin •

WALES

ENGLAND
• Manchester
London •

ENGLISH CHANNEL

1 English Channel
2 North Sea
3 Thames
4 Saunton Sands
5 Harlyn
6 Newquay
7 Hythe
8 Weymouth
9 Isle of Wight
10 West Wittering
11 Hayling Island

the wind is from the north. The Hayling seafront launch is less sheltered, but at low tide it also offers relatively smooth water. At midtide the water is choppy, but at high tide the shore break (the surf at water's edge) can be rough. The prevailing southwesterly wind is side-onshore to the beach.

At West Wittering the prevailing southwesterly wind is dead onshore, so launching can be difficult. However, there are sandbars that block and deflect the swell, so launching in the southwesterly wind is possible and wave riding can be good, particularly at midtide. Sailing is best at Wittering when the wind is out of the northwest and blows sideshore to the beach and the surf. As at Hayling, low tide offers the mildest conditions, while high tide is for experts only when the surf is large.

Both venues offer ample parking space and windsurfing shops nearby; however, they can be extremely crowded on weekends.

To the southeast of London is the small town of Hythe. It's a short distance away from the busy ferry traffic of Dover and Folkestone but still lies at one of the nearest points to France. On a clear day, you can easily see across the channel. Some of the best sailing at Hythe occurs in the late summer and early fall, when the water is still reasonably warm and the southwesterly winds blow for days at a time.

Farther to the west, just past Bournemouth, is the town of Weymouth, the site of many sailing and windsurfing speed trials. Speed trials are sailing events in which boats and boards try to sail a straight measured course as quickly as possible. The Weymouth area is particularly good for these trials because Portland Bill, a low isthmus of land on the west side of Weymouth Bay, keeps the water flat and well protected, while allowing the wind to blow past unimpeded. Advanced windsurfers sailing in the harbor can enjoy the sensation of flying across nearly flat water at speeds of 35, 40, and even 45 mph (58, 67, and 75 kph). In the meantime, novices can safely sail in the area because the waters are so well protected and enclosed.

The Isle of Wight has windy weather year-round and reasonably warm temperatures in the summer.

Exploring Western Europe

Europe has every bit as long and varied a coastline as North America, so windsurfing sites are abundant. Europe is farther north, however, so the warm season isn't as long as it is in parts of North America, and the winds tend to be more erratic. The waters of the Baltic and North Sea tend to be cool or cold for most of the year, as do those of the Atlantic. The Mediterranean Sea and some inland lakes warm up in the summer, but the humid warmth found in the southeastern U.S. and Caribbean is largely absent from European windsurfing sites. Still, with the help of a wetsuit,

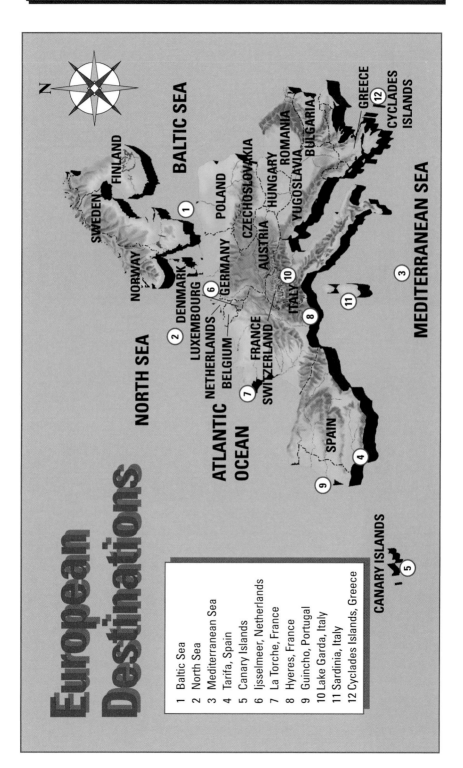

European Destinations

1 Baltic Sea
2 North Sea
3 Mediterranean Sea
4 Tarifa, Spain
5 Canary Islands
6 Ijsselmeer, Netherlands
7 La Torche, France
8 Hyeres, France
9 Guincho, Portugal
10 Lake Garda, Italy
11 Sardinia, Italy
12 Cyclades Islands, Greece

CANARY ISLANDS

NORTH SEA

ATLANTIC OCEAN

BALTIC SEA

MEDITERRANEAN SEA

NORWAY
SWEDEN
FINLAND
DENMARK
NETHERLANDS
LUXEMBOURG
BELGIUM
GERMANY
POLAND
CZECHOSLOVAKIA
AUSTRIA
HUNGARY
ROMANIA
YUGOSLAVIA
BULGARIA
GREECE
CYCLADES ISLANDS
FRANCE
SWITZERLAND
ITALY
SPAIN

N

Windsurfing at Lake Garda can be serene and relaxing.

anyone can enjoy the varied conditions and unique cultural experiences of windsurfing in Europe.

LAKE GARDA

Midway between Milan and Venice, on the southern fringe of the Italian Alps, lies Lake Garda, the most popular windsurfing site in Europe. Garda is much like the Columbia River Gorge: It's surrounded by mountains and is heavily populated by windsurfers during the summer season. The towns of Riva and Torbole at the north end of the lake are the focus of windsurfing activity, much as Hood River is the focus in the gorge. The scene in these towns is much like that of a ski resort, with waterside restaurants and hotels. Windsurfers vacation here as much for the ambiance as for the sailing.

Accommodations include hotels and campsites in and near the towns. Another good place to stay is the Hotel Pier, a short distance south of Torbole, where the wind is strongest and most consistent.

The appeal of Lake Garda, other than the spectacular mountain scenery and hiking trails, is the reliable wind. During normal summer weather, there's a brisk downslope flow of cool air from the mountains to the north toward the valley to the south early each morning. By midmorning this flow has usually ceased and the lake is calm. By afternoon, however, the heating of the mountains reverses the flow of air and causes a southerly thermal wind to blow for the remainder of the day.

TARIFA

Tarifa lies on the southernmost tip of Spain, where the Mediterranean Sea and Atlantic Ocean meet. It is a short distance west of Gibraltar and less than 10 miles (16 km) north of Africa. This arid, windblown outpost enjoys more than 3,000 hours per year of sun, which makes it one of the sunniest places in Spain. There are rainy periods in the fall and winter, but the temperature rarely falls below 50 degrees Fahrenheit (10 degrees Celsius) in the winter, and averages about 77 degrees Fahrenheit (25 degrees Celsius) in the summer. Tarifa has come into its own as a destination for expert windsurfers and a venue for one of the biggest speedsailing events in the world. There's not much in the way of beach bars and tourist traps, as the windsurfers who visit Tarifa are serious about sailing.

Tarifa experiences two main wind directions: east and west. The easterly, called the Levante, blows mainly in the summer and fall and can be very strong (25 to 45 mph, or 40 to 75 kph). A good place to sail with the Levante blowing is near the island of Palomas. The westerly wind, called the Poniente, tends to blow at about 10 to 30 mph (16 to 48 kph) and is best between Casa Porros and Punta Paloma.

THE CANARIES

Spain's Canary Islands, which lie between 50 and 250 miles (80 to 400 km) off the west coast of Africa, are the "Hawaii" of Europe. These are volcanic islands similar in height to the islands of Hawaii and Maui but on the whole

Riding a clean little wave like this one in the Canaries is one of life's greatest pleasures.

much more arid. The water is cooler than the waters of Hawaii, and the waves are less impressive. Still, the winds are reliable, especially in the summer, and windsurfing resort operations here are among the best in the world.

The most popular beaches are on the northeasternmost island of Lanzarote and the southernmost part of Gran Canaria. They offer flat to moderately choppy water. The island of Fuerteventura between Gran Canaria and Lanzarote offers good wave sailing at the north end in the winter and hosts an international speedsailing competition every summer at the south end.

OTHER DESTINATIONS

Starkly missing from the list above are dozens of terrific windsurfing sites in Holland, France, and other countries. The Ijsselmeer, a lake in the north of Holland, offers protected, flat-water windsurfing; La Torche, near Quimper in Brittany, and Hyeres, on the Mediterranean, east of Toulon, are France's most renowned World Cup windsurfing venues; Portugal has Guincho, Italy has Sardinia, Greece has the Cyclades Islands to the southeast of Athens. These are all spectacular places to windsurf.

Australia and New Zealand

Australia and New Zealand provide conditions as varied and inviting as any windsurfing area in the world.

Australia is as large as the 48 coterminous states of the U.S., yet has a population of only about 15 million. Much of the continent is desert, so much of Australia's population lives on the relatively wet east and southeast coastal areas in cities such as Sydney and Melbourne.

According to Michael McGrath, editor of *Freesail* magazine, the Australian coastline is an endless progression of golden sandy beaches, among which it's nearly impossible to choose. However, good places for novice and intermediate windsurfers in the Sydney area are Balmoral Beach and Rose Bay. Both are on Sydney Harbor and exposed to the prevailing summer northeasterlies. North of the city are Pittwater Bay, Palm Beach, and the huge Lake Macquarie; to the south is Botany Bay—all good for beginning and intermediate windsurfers.

The most famous of Sydney's ocean beaches is Long Beach, which has good wind and surf frequently during the summer. South of Sydney, though, is Gerroa, the beach with the most reliable sea breeze. Even farther south, near Melbourne, is Port Phillip Bay, which has good conditions for all types of windsurfers, and Point Danger, which is an experts-only surf beach.

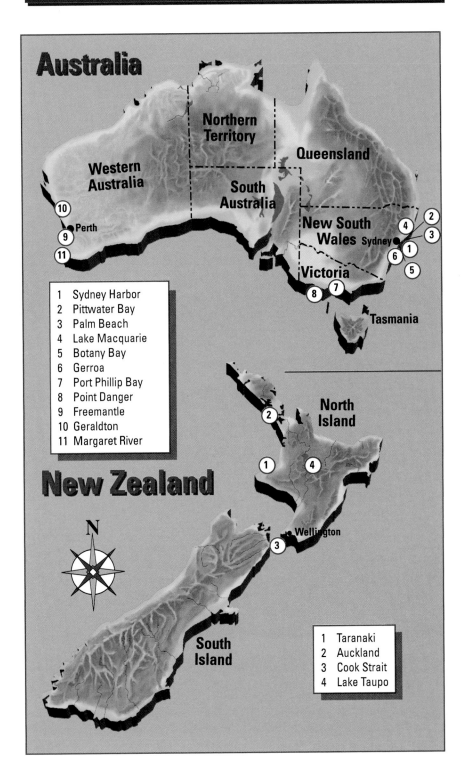

Australia

Northern Territory

Queensland

Western Australia

South Australia

New South Wales   Sydney

10

Perth

9

11

Victoria

1   Sydney Harbor
2   Pittwater Bay
3   Palm Beach
4   Lake Macquarie
5   Botany Bay
6   Gerroa
7   Port Phillip Bay
8   Point Danger
9   Freemantle
10 Geraldton
11 Margaret River

4

2

3

6

1

5

8

7

Tasmania

New Zealand

N

North Island

2

1

4

Wellington

3

South Island

1   Taranaki
2   Auckland
3   Cook Strait
4   Lake Taupo

With spectacular windsurfing conditions and a strong orientation toward watersports, it's not surprising that Australia sends more pros to the World Cup than any other country.

As good as eastern Australia's windsurfing can be, western Australia is the destination for most hardcore windsurfers because of the strong, consistent sea breeze that blows there in the summer. Freemantle, near Perth, on the southwest coast of Western Australia, offers both wave sailing on the Indian Ocean and flat-water sailing on the Swan River. Nearby are legendary wave sailing spots Geraldton and Margaret River.

New Zealand, south of Australia, is smack in the middle of what sailors call the "roaring forties," the strong westerly winds that circle the earth between 40 and 50 degrees south latitude. New Zealand's exposed position means that the ocean water is generally cool and rough. Indeed, some of the windiest wave sailing conditions exist in Taranaki, on the west coast of New Zealand's northern island, halfway between Auckland and Wellington. In fact, Kiwis who have been to Maui and sailed at Ho'okipa claim that Taranaki is in the same league.

More protected waters can be found near Auckland, and some of the windiest waters in the world lie in Cook Strait between the north and south islands, near Wellington.

For less intimidating freshwater sailing, there's Lake Taupo in the middle of the north island. At a size of 30 square kilometers (11 square miles), Lake Taupo is the largest lake in New Zealand. Alternatively, any of the numerous alpine lakes on the south island provide good freshwater sailing as well.

Other places in the general area of the southwestern Pacific, like Fiji, Okinawa, the Mariana Islands, and New Caledonia offer trade winds, warm waters, and, in some cases, good wave sailing. For example, Cocos Island, at the south end of the island of Guam in the Marianas, borders Cocos Lagoon, a shallow, windswept, flat-water lagoon completely surrounded by barrier reef. It's a marvelous place for beginner and expert windsurfers alike. Likewise, New Caledonia is a World Cup race venue and home to some of the world's top pros. It offers consistent trade winds and protected waters.

6

PURSUING WINDSURFING FURTHER

Suppose you're a tennis player.

How much time would you spend hitting a tennis ball against a wall? If you're like most people, the wall's not going to keep you interested for long. Pretty soon you're going to want to play with a person—volley a little or play a game. Likewise in windsurfing. After a while you're going to want to play with other people, not just chat with them on the beach or wave to them as you sail past on the water, but actually do stuff with them—interact—on the water.

Games such as tag, chase, buoyball, freestyle, and racing are great ways to enjoy windsurfing and have good times with others. They're the next step after you get the basics figured out, and they help you master all those board- and sail-handling skills you need to progress in the sport.

Tag

The simplest windsurfing game is tag. Played most often on longboards in light winds, it's little different from the playground game and requires no great skill. In its most common version, there's a player designated to be *It* who must try to tag one of the other players by bumping boards. All players must stay within a reasonably confined area marked by buoys or land, and immediate tag-backs are not allowed.

A variation on tag that works well when a single player is having trouble making a tag involves two players being *It*. They can work together to make tags.

Most modern boards are not well suited to tag. They turn slowly, have cluttered decks that interfere with quick footwork, quickly become dangerously fast as the wind increases, and are often too fragile for the game. A board like the kneesurfer, on the other hand, is good for tag. It's soft, slow, maneuverable, impervious to damage from collisions, and virtually incapable of injuring players.

Chase

Chase can be played on any kind of board in any conditions. Set two buoys a short distance apart along a line oriented perpendicular to the wind direction. The distance between them may be about 10 yards (or meters) when the wind is light, or around 100 to 200 yards (or meters) when the wind is high. In any case, the buoys should be far enough apart that it takes the players at least 10 seconds to sail from one buoy to the other.

Two players start sailing simultaneously, each at a different buoy. Each sails continuous circuits or figure eights around the buoys, trying to catch the other. They can jibe around both buoys, tack around both, or alternate tacks with jibes. As long as both players sail the same course, the game will work. A game ends when the nose of one board catches up to the tail of the other.

For a more demanding course, set the buoys along a line oriented parallel with the wind direction. Just about any orientation will do, and the more variations you try, the better your sailing skills will become.

Buoyball

Windsurfing is generally not thought of as a team sport. However, a waterborne cross between half-court basketball and soccer, buoyball, has been played on Windsurfers for years. Buoyball is a light-wind, longboard game that, given the limitations of modern longboards, is probably best played on something like a kneesurfer or a lightwind-oriented longboard.

The buoyball "court" consists of a goal, two buoys set about 5 yards (or meters) apart on a line perpendicular to the wind direction, and a clearing buoy set about 30 to 50 yards (or meters) directly downwind of the goal.

The ball can be a child's inflatable bouncing toy—the kind with a handle molded onto it. However, such balls tend to rest ring-down in the water. An alternative that's easier to pick up is a ringless ball, similar in size and weight to the bouncing toy, encased in netting. There are two teams consisting of three to six players each.

To begin play, a member of the team that won the coin toss picks up the ball, sails just downwind of the clearing buoy, and begins sailing upwind toward the goal. The ball carrier may retain possession or throw the ball to a teammate. However, when the board of an opposing team member contacts the board of the ball carrier, the carrier must drop the ball. Having dropped the ball, the former carrier may not touch it again until after someone else has handled it.

To score, a player must throw (3 points) or sail (5 points) the ball over the goal line. A member of the team that is scored against takes possession of the ball and begins another round by sailing downwind of the clearing buoy. The first team to score 20 points wins.

Freestyle

Longboard freestyle is a type of windsurfing that was once quite popular. Major longboard freestyle championship events were staged in the mid-1970s through mid-1980s, and freestyle was even a demonstration event at the 1984 summer Olympics. Interest has waned in recent years, at least in part because the sharp rails, slowness to turn, deck clutter, and, in many cases, fragility of modern longboards leave most windsurfers with equipment ill-suited for freestyle.

Still, longboard freestyle is good light-wind fun, especially if you can lay your hands on an old Windsurfer, Mistral Competition, or a similar board. You can have a grand time doing pirouettes, railrides, wheelies, and dozens of other tricks.

The freestyle most popular nowadays is shortboard wave and bump performance. This sort of sailing is highly athletic and requires a lot of wind. It's also the most spectacular form of windsurfing. Shortboard performers can do jumps, flips, and loops in the air and nearly any amazing trick you can imagine on the water.

Light-wind freestyle can improve your flexibility and hone your sense of balance to a sharp edge.

For more information, consult the numerous books and videos devoted to all types of freestyle and wave performance.

Racing

Racing. The word brings to some minds visions of armor-clad gladiators driving chariots of death. Others think of humorless nerds grimly jockeying for position on a starting line. Of course, some racers *are* too rough and others too serious. However, most often racing is just another game and need be no more serious.

If you like casual, racing can be as casual as a couple of windsurfers pointing to a buoy on the water and saying "race ya," like a couple of kids running for the kitchen door. If you like structure, formal races have plenty of rules and traditions. In either case, formal or casual, racing is the best way to improve your windsurfing skills. It gives you feedback on how you're doing, motivation to do better, and, through observing fellow competitors, sources of information about how to improve.

Unfortunately, in recent years much racing has been an exhausting equipment battle, with competitors forced to buy new boards and sails every year. That's because the PBA World Cup has no limitations on equipment, and too many club-level races have adopted this approach—never mind that you have to spend the price of an expensive car to be fully equipped for this kind of racing. Even by yacht-racing standards, this sort of racing is expensive.

The more interesting style of racing, if you don't have an unlimited budget, is not trying to go as fast as humanly possible but trying to go fast on the same equipment as the next person, and, more important, trying to sail a shorter distance around the course than the others. Going faster than the next person involves many issues of equipment adjustment and technique. These are familiar concepts, roughly equivalent to tuning a car well and doing a better job of driving it around the track at Indy. Sailing a shorter distance around the course, however, is not such a familiar concept to most people. On the face of it, it sounds like cheating. Certainly, if you were to drive only 499 miles of the Indy 500, you wouldn't win. How can you sail a shorter distance and win a windsurfing race?

Racing is about doing stuff with other windsurfers *while* you're windsurfing.

The answer has to do with the fact that boards don't travel directly from the downwind mark to the upwind mark of the course. They have to zigzag back and forth. If the wind shifts during that zigging and zagging (which it always does), some boards will be able to sail better angles, hence shorter distances, on some of those zigzags, while others end up sailing worse angles and greater distances. The biggest trick in racing under sail, then, is to figure out what the wind is about to do so that you can sail a shorter distance to the next mark. As no one can predict future wind precisely, every decision is a throw of the dice. An informed throw, of course, but dice nonetheless.

This backgammon-like quality of racing is the one that makes it so interesting. You can be far in the lead but quickly find yourself in the middle of the pack after missing a wind shift. Or, you can be trailing the fleet, spot a wind shift before the others, and be in the lead within minutes.

Drag racing is a popular pastime for advanced- to pro-level slalom sailors.

Some of the best racing is on the slowest boards because they can turn quickly and take the most advantage of small variations in the wind. Thus, boards as simple as the kneesurfer are as good for racing as the latest, most exotic speed machines. Similarity, not speed, is the key. For that reason, one design racing, in which every board in a race fleet is virtually identical to the next, has proven immensely popular. Fortunately, it still exists in windsurfing in the form of the IMCO One Design class.

For more information about the IMCO One Design, contact the International Mistral Class Organization or your national sailing federation. For more information on racing in general, consult books and videos on both dinghy and board racing.

Speed Checks

A speed check, a race against the clock rather than against other windsurfers, involves repeated solo passes through a speed trap. Participants don't have to be able to turn, or jibe, or cross a starting line at precisely the right moment. They only have to sail in a straight line for 100 yards or so (or meters).

The real hook in speed traps is that they usually include a digital display that shows your speed at the end of each pass. Make that first run and you can't stop. You always finish one pass thinking you can do better on the next, and of course you can, because the feedback from the display helps you learn to sail faster. A good day of speed sailing can mean dozens of passes per competitor, with everyone sailing faster, in better balance, and with greater ease.

WINDSURFING THROUGH LIFE

I bought my first board late in the winter of 1975. Since then, I've owned countless toys and tried countless sports, but I keep returning to windsurfing. Why? Does windsurfing really have something special, or am I crazy?

Sure, there's the exercise you can get doing it. In 1994, the coach of the Hong Kong windsurfing team did a study and concluded that sailing a typical Olympic-style race was as strenuous as competing in a triathlon. Of course, you only get that kind of workout if you put some effort into it, but that's true in every sport. Nothing special there.

Then, there's the mental challenge of windsurfing. If you're a wave sailor, you're always assessing and reacting to a complex, rapidly changing environment: reading a wave, predicting how and when it's going to break, then adjusting your path to meet it at the point of maximum kinetic and potential energy. Or if you race, you're dealing with thinking, striving human competitors. You're watching the wind, making adjustments, watching other racers adjust, meeting their challenge, striving to do better for the sheer pleasure of striving. Of course, bashing the lip of a thick, juicy wave is something you can do in surfing, and competing against your buddies in a friendly race is hardly unique to windsurfing. What's so different?

A lot of windsurfers rhapsodize about the sun on their face, the wind at their back, the sparkling turquoise water blurring beneath their feet. They write poems of spray and saltwater and flying fish leaping and gliding along beside them. They sing of surfing waves, riding the wind, skimming like a seagull across swells and over whitecaps. It's all special, of course, but plenty of sports can bring you close to nature.

The question remains: What's so special about windsurfing? You'd think I'd know after 20 years of doing it. But maybe that's it—that I still *can* do it after 20 years; that it hasn't pounded and ground my joints into paste and left me broken and spent at age 40; that it provides the kind of physical activity that slows aging rather than speeds it up the way some sports do. And maybe the combination of the physical benefits with the mental challenge—the sort of challenge that keeps me learning and eager for more after 20 years—maybe that's it. Of course, a few other sports have those elements, but do they combine them with the thrill of speed and the sensuous pleasures of warm sand, hot sun, and cool water? No way. It's this rare combination of qualities that makes windsurfing special. You'll see.

APPENDIX

FOR MORE INFORMATION

Organizations

British Windsurfing Association
3 Newburgh St.
London W1V 1LH
UK
(71) 439 1037; fax (71) 287 0973

 The BWA is the windsurfing branch of the Royal Yachting Association, which is the national governing body for sailing in the U.K.

Canadian Yachting Association
1600 James Naismith Dr., Ste. 504
Gloucester, ON K1B 5N4
Canada
(613) 748-5687; fax (613) 748-5688

 The national governing body for sailing in Canada. Windsurfing Canada is the branch of the CYA devoted to windsurfing issues.

International Mistral Class Association
c/o M1 Sport Technik GmbH
Forststrasse 2
D-85655 Grosschelfendorf
Germany
(80) 95 6420; fax (80) 95 6429

    The association of the Mistral One Design.

International Yacht Racing Union
60 Knightsbridge
London, SW1
UK
(71) 928 6611; fax (71) 401 8301

    The international governing body for the sport of sailing.

New South Wales Wavesailing Association
c/o Gary McEvoy
4/54 Seaview St.
Cronulla, NSW 2230
Australia
(02) 523 0225

    One of Australia's numerous windsurfing associations.

Professional Boardsailors Association
Gibbs House, Kennel Ride
Ascot, Berks SL5 7NT
UK
(34) 488 3020

    The international organizing and sanctioning body for professional windsurfing events.

Stormriders Sailboard Club
P.O. Box 375
Narrabeen, NSW 2101
Australia
(02) 972 1315

    Another one of Australia's many windsurfing associations.

U.S. Sailing Association
P.O. Box 209
Newport, RI 02840
(401) 849-5200; fax (401) 849-5208

The national governing body for the sport of sailing in the U.S.

United States Windsurfing Association
P.O. Box 978
Hood River, OR 97031
(503) 386-8708; fax (503) 386-2108

The USWA addresses water access and water quality issues and organizes regattas. It is a branch of U.S. Sailing.

Books

A Beginner's Guide to Zen and the Art of Windsurfing, by Frank Fox. Oakland, CA: Amber, 1988.

A light and highly readable guide for novice, intermediate, and advanced windsurfers.

Championship Tactics, by Gary Jobson and Tom Whidden. New York: Saint Martin's Press, 1990.

Aimed at sailboat racers, this is nevertheless a good guide to many of the tactical and strategic situations racing windsurfers will encounter.

Freestyle Windsurfing With Gary Eversole, by Roger Jones. San Francisco: Harper & Row, 1983.

A comprehensive guide to freestyle windsurfing.

Start Windsurfing Right, by James Coutts. St. Louis: Mosby–Year Book, 1991.

A thorough, basic introduction to the theory, mechanics, and safety considerations of windsurfing.

Wind and Strategy, by Stuart Walker. New York: Norton, 1973.

Aimed at dinghy racers but good for anyone interested in highly localized wind phenomena and their effects on sailing craft.

Wind Strategy (2nd ed.), by David Houghton. New York: State Mutual, 1990.

Designed to teach racing sailors about small-scale wind shifts and velocity fluctuations.

Periodicals

American Windsurfer
Grapho Inc.
Bayview Business Park
Gilford, NH 03246
USA
(800) 292-2772; fax (603) 293-2723

This is a large-format, artistic magazine that focuses on the people of windsurfing.

Freesail
P.O. Box 746
Darlinghurst, NSW 2010
Australia
(02) 331 5006; fax (02) 360 5367

Australia's leading windsurfing magazine.

New England Windsurfing Journal
P.O. Box 2120
Southbury, CT 06488
USA
(203) 264-9463; fax (203) 264-9467

A tabloid-format, newsprint-quality monthly about windsurfing people and events from Maine to North Carolina.

Boards
196 Eastern Esplinade
Southend-On-Sea, Essex
England SS1 3AB
01702 582245; fax 01702 588434

Britain's best-selling windsurfing magazine attracts an international audience to its articles on technique, equipment, and travel.

Windsport
2409 Marine Cr.
Oakville, ON L6L 1Z6
Canada
(416) 698-0138; fax (416) 698-8080

Canada's windsurfing magazine focuses on equipment, technique, events, and travel.

WindSurfing
P.O. Box 8500
Winter Park, FL 32790
USA
(407) 628-4802; fax (407) 628-7061

The leading windsurfing magazine in the U.S., *WindSurfing* focuses on equipment, technique, and travel in its full-color format.

WindTracks
P.O. Box 62
Pistol River, OR 97444
USA
(503) 247-4153; fax (503) 247-7556

The soul of high-wind windsurfing in the U.S.

Instructional Videos

The Carving Jibe, The Waterstart, The Step Jibe, The Stance
Five-time world champion Rhonda Smith takes viewers through intermediate and advanced skills in four 20-minute videos.

Get the Kids On Board
This video covers most aspects of teaching children how to windsurf.

Shortboard Sailing Techniques I and II
This video teaches basic through expert shortboard skills, including jumping.

Starting Point
An introductory video.

Towards the Limit

Advanced tricks and techniques: Basic jumping and landing, jump jibes, board 360s, etc.

Turning Point

A guide to basic planing skills such as footstrap use and high-speed jibing.

Winning Streak

How to win windsurfing races.

Other Sources of Information

America Online
8619 Westwood Center Dr.
Vienna, VA 22182
(800) 827-6364; fax (800) 827-4595

This is a computer on-line service that offers both a windsurfing forum and access to the Internet.

CompuServe
P.O. Box 20212
Columbus, OH 43220
USA
(800) 848-8990

CompuServe is a computer on-line service that maintains a windsurfing forum.

Delphi Internet Services
1030 Massachusetts Ave.
Cambridge, MA 02138
USA
(800) 695-4005; fax (617) 491-6642

Delphi is a computer on-line service that offers Internet access.

The Internet

The Internet is a network of computer networks that circles the globe. Windsurfers from all over the world with Internet access are able to pose questions and participate in discussion about windsurfing by entering the "rec.windsurfing" area. The Internet has no address, but you can gain access to it via on-line services such as America Online and Delphi.

The Wind Hot Line
422 Sugar Dr.
Bolton, MA 01740
(800) 765-4253; fax (508) 779-2860

This is a windsurfing-oriented wind forecast service with wind sensors in all Atlantic coast states from North Carolina to Maine.

WindSight
319 SW Washington St., # 909
Portland, OR 97024
(503) 227-7455; fax (503) 227-1101

This is a windsurfing-oriented wind forecast service with sensors in the Columbia River Gorge, the Oregon coast, the Seattle area, the San Francisco Bay area, and Maui.

WINDSURFING LINGO

battens—Rods or tubes that are built into a sail and used to control its shape.

beam reach—A point of sail perpendicular to the wind direction.

beating to windward—Taking a zigzag course and sailing as quickly as possible in an upwind direction.

boardsailing—An alternative way to say "windsurfing."

boom—The part of the rig that the windsurfer grasps while in a normal sailing position.

broad reach—A point of sail between beam reach and run.

bump sailing—Windsurfing in high winds and choppy water.

camber inducer—A plastic part that fits in the luff sleeve of a sail between the front of a batten and the mast and keeps the batten at a uniform distance from the mast.

capping—Said of water that has white caps. Capping begins to occur at wind speeds of about 10 mph (16 kph).

centerboard—The wing-shaped composite or wood plank that projects below or rests retracted within a longboard. It keeps the board from sliding excessively sideways.

clew—The corner of the sail that ties to the back end of the boom.

close hauled—A point of sail in which the board is pointed as much in an upwind direction as possible while still maintaining good speed through the water.

close reach—A point of sail between beating and beam reach.

downhaul line—The line that attaches the bottom corner of the sail (the tack of the sail) to the mast base.

downwind—The direction in which the wind is blowing.

eye of the wind—The precise direction from which the wind is blowing.

gust—A sudden, brief increase in wind strength.

high wind—Wind blowing at more than 20 mph (33 kph).

hull—A windsurfing board exclusive of rig.

jibe—Turning around in such a way that the tail of the board passes through the eye of the wind.

knots—Nautical miles per hour. A nautical mile is 2,000 yards (1,850 meters), and knots is the standard unit of speed for water- and aircraft.

light wind—Wind blowing at roughly between 0 and 10 mph (0 to 16 kph).

lightly powered—The condition of having a small sail or little wind. The sail generates little power.

longboard—Any board equipped with a centerboard.

luff—(noun) The leading or front edge of a sail—the part the wind normally strikes first; (verb) To "sheet out," or reduce the sail's angle of incidence to the wind to the point where the wind no longer fills out the front of the sail.

lull—A sudden, brief decrease in wind strength.

mast—The fiberglass, aluminum, or carbon fiber pole that fits in the luff of the sail.

moderate wind—Wind blowing at roughly 11 to 20 mph (17 to 32 kph).

moderately powered—The condition of having a big enough sail and enough wind to make planing barely possible.

nose—The front end of a board.

offshore wind—Wind that blows from land to water.

one design—The name of the Olympic windsurfing class. More generally, a one design class is one in which all boards are virtually identical.

outhaul—The line that attaches the clew of the sail to the back end of the boom.

overpowered—The condition that occurs when the sail is too big for the windsurfer in the prevailing wind and sea conditions.

plane—To skim over the water rather than plow through it.

port—The left side of a board when looking forward.

port tack—A board is on port tack when the sailor's left hand (in its normal sailing position) is the one nearer the mast.

powered—The condition of having a big enough sail and enough wind to easily plane.

pumping—Flapping the sail the way a bird flaps its wings. Used to gain speed.

rail—(noun) The side of a board; (verb) To rail a board is to tilt it to one side.

reach—A point of sail that is neither close hauled nor running.

rig—The combination of mast, boom, sail, mast base, and universal joint. Everything above the deck of the board. To rig is to put windsurfing gear together.

running—Sailing directly downwind.

sailboard—The equipment on which one windsurfs.

sheet in—To catch the wind with the sail.

slalom—A type of shortboard designed to go fast in moderate or high wind. A type of race.

starboard—The right side of the board when looking forward.

starboard tack—A board is on starboard tack when the sailor's right hand (in its normal sailing position) is the one nearer the mast.

tack—(noun) The lower corner of the sail; (verb) To change direction of travel so that the nose of the board passes through the eye of the wind (opposite of *jibe*).

tail—Back end of board.

universal joint—The flexible rubber or mechanical device that attaches the rig to the board while allowing the two to turn and tilt independently.

unsheet—To spill the wind from the sail.

uphaul—(noun) The rope used to lift the rig from the water; (verb) To lift the sail from the water by pulling on the uphaul rope.

upwind—The direction from which the wind is blowing.

volume—The amount of water a board would displace if totally submerged, usually given in liters.

waterstart—Setting sail in such a way that the windsurfer is lifted from the water by the force of the wind on the sail.

whitecaps—The white tops of wind-driven waves. Whitecaps begin to appear when the wind is gusting to about 10 mph (16 kph).

windshift—A change in wind direction.

windsurfer—(a) A person who windsurfs; (b) a sailboard.

INDEX

PHOTO CREDITS

ABOUT THE AUTHOR

Ken Winner has been involved in the sport and business of windsurfing since 1975. Not only has he competed and won at all levels, but he also has influenced the evolution of windsurfing equipment and technique. His career as one of the first professional windsurfers involved competing worldwide and working with equipment manufacturers to develop better equipment for recreational windsurfers.

Since retiring from pro competition in 1986, Winner has continued to promote the sport of windsurfing. He helped revive the United States Windsurfing Association, the windsurfing arm of U.S. Sailing, and served as its president in 1987 and 1988. Recently he has written extensively for *WindSurfing* magazine on the topics of equipment and technique.

Winner, his wife, Alison Fitts, and their children live in White Salmon, WA.